How to Lose the Wrong Guy ...
Without Losing You

How to Lose the Wrong Guy...
Without Losing You

Renee Medema

R.Y.M. Publishing

Interior design by Meadowlark Publishing Services.

ISBN 978-0-9995223-1-8

Published by R.Y.M. Publishing. Manufactured in the United States of America.

Published 2018

To God, who gave me life and a purpose.

To my parents, who raised me to be the person I am today and inspired me to become whatever I dreamed I could be. With love and encouragement, they supported me to never give up regardless of the obstacles that stand in the way, and grounded me with faith in God that has been my foundation.

To Mary Kelly (aka my "career mom"), who saw something in me that I had not yet realized, and molded and shaped that potential into something tangible. She supported me, with wisdom and courage, to step into the unknown and to further develop my potential. She encouraged me to not let others intimidate me and to not hinder my own success. She has a unique perspective on the world and her sharing that with me has expanded my own world exponentially.

And to Andrés Tapia, who inspired me to bring this book to life. The idea of writing a book had been brewing in my mind for years, and he encouraged me and guided me on the "how to," which made it possible. He believed in me and made me believe in myself. I owe the title of this book to his creativity and the outline and overall flow to his writer's genius.

Contents

Contents

Acknowledgments

I want to thank all of the strong women in my life who have encouraged me, supported me, and held me accountable to never settle for less than I deserve.

Thank you to my grandmothers, who were both strong women; even though they grew up during a time when women were not allowed to have a voice, they never let my grandfathers walk all over them. They have been an inspiration to me, and following their example, I am now a strong woman too. The wealth of knowledge I gained from them during our second Saturdays together will be forever engrained in me.

I regret not having spent similar time with my grandfathers, who passed within six weeks of each other, but this motivated me to not lose out on any more time with my grandmothers. The silver lining of my grandfathers' deaths was realizing the value our elders bring to our lives, and I am grateful to have been given those cherished moments. I'm a different person today because of the quality time I was able to spend with my grandmothers.

I'm so appreciative to all you strong women in my life who were brave enough to share your stories with me and other women. I couldn't have written this book without you, and I know that your heartaches and lessons learned will offer eye-opening reasons for other women to never settle for less. I know that every bad relationship you've had with all the wrong guys and the stories you have told will help other women learn from those experiences—and hopefully never have to suffer through similar situations themselves.

Thank you, Lori, for being the best friend I could ask for and for all your love and encouragement over the past twenty-five years. You've always believed in me, encouraged me, and told me how proud you are of everything I've accomplished. I'm so proud of you too. You are an amazing mother, a wonderful wife, and an extraordinary friend. You're sentimental in ways I will never be, but I love you so much because of it. I can't tell you how grateful I am that you've always been there for me any time I needed you.

Thank you, Denise, for being a wonderful sister, teaching me to love me first, and motivating me to move out of state and get my degree.

To the strong women I attended college with who juggled full-time jobs, full-time coursework, and their families … you motivated me to do more than I could have otherwise done. You inspired me and impressed me with your ability to accomplish so much. Your determination and resolve definitely made me realize I have so much more potential in me.

I'll forever be grateful for my experiences attending college at Roosevelt University. I love that the university is founded on equality and that social justice is interwoven into every class in some way. My professors were instrumental in educating me and shaping my views to see the world differently. During my studies, I was able to see how far we are from having a nation undivided where justice rules. With renewed hope and fight, I will continue to share with others the importance of equality, acceptance, diversity, open-mindedness, and inclusion in our lives.

Introduction

I pick up the phone ... "Hey, how are you?"

I hear uncontrollable sobbing and a broken, barely audible voice. "We had a fight again. He stormed out and said it was over for real this time. Why won't he just answer me? I mean I just want to talk to him to make sure everything is okay." I hear more sobbing ...

I pause and then ask "What did you fight about?"

"I don't even know. Everything seemed to be good. We were having a relaxing night at home and I mentioned something about a few nights ago when it took him four hours to answer my text. That night I had asked him what took him so long, but he never answered me and it was bothering me. He's done it before and my gut is telling me that he might be cheating, but I don't know for sure. I brought it up so I could see if he would give me a solid answer this time and he completely overreacted. He got off the couch and told me if I didn't trust him, then we couldn't be together. He told me I never give him any space and I always accuse him of doing something wrong. He said that he felt he couldn't catch a break and no matter how hard he tried it was never good enough for me. Then he said if he wanted to be with anyone else, he would just leave me. He said 'I told you I would never cheat on you, but I am tired of trying to prove myself and it might be better if we take a break.' Then he left."

I say, "You've had fights like this in the past. Just give him a little time to cool down. He'll come back."

I can hear in her voice that she's fighting back the tears … "What if something happened to him?"

I say, "He's fine. He probably just went for a drive or maybe went to the gym to work out."

Then I hear the words I was dreading to hear: "I honestly don't know what I would do without him. Maybe I am too hard on him. I know he's going through a lot right now, but he is a really good guy. I probably don't give him enough space. It's just that I love him so much and want to be with him all the time."

I wish I had only heard this story once, but I've heard it over and over again from too many of my girlfriends. It's unfortunate that sometimes we allow guys to manipulate us into believing something that isn't true. It's also unfortunate that 99 percent of the time in a scenario like this, the guy is cheating.

I'm not a relationship expert, but I have seen enough

women settle for less than they deserve and I feel obligated to share what I have learned. I don't want to pass up an opportunity to impart knowledge and wisdom that may help other women. I've done my best to live my life without regret. I've made mistakes and enjoyed successes, but I've always tried to live life to its fullest and avoid the possibility of looking back at any situation and saying "if only" or "I wish I had." This mentality has allowed me to step out and take chances I may not have been willing to take otherwise.

Although I didn't know the first thing about writing a book, I didn't let my ignorance stop me. I researched, resourced, and set my mind to make it happen. I encourage you to "carpe diem" and seize this moment in your life to decide that you will no longer settle, you won't let obstacles stand in your way, and you will live life every day like it's your last.

I hope you enjoy and learn from this collection of stories, advice, experiences, and recommendations. Some of the stories are my own, some are my alter ego's, some are from friends, and some are embellished just for fun. The important thing to note is that the entire collection highlights elements that are truthful and useful in any dating scenario or long-term relationship. I want to be able to share simple truths that will be relevant and helpful but will not hurt any real people who have gone through some hurtful and unfortunate experiences. Therefore, I've changed some names to protect the innocent.

1

My Story

Wrong guys are all over the place. They work in our offices, they live in our apartment buildings, and they work out with us at the gym. They walk their dogs at the same dog parks, attend services with us where we worship, buy groceries at our local grocers, and go to the same restaurants, bars, and nightclubs. They live in our world, and at some point in our lives there is a good chance we will encounter one. The problem is that they don't wear labels. They don't have red flags, obviously displayed, to let us know that they are the wrong guys.

I know because I have met plenty of them, and I have had my heart broken many times because of empty promises these wrong guys made.

Just to be clear, wrong guys aren't *bad* guys. They

may be perfectly suited for other women, but they aren't suited for us and that's what makes them "wrong." Very few men will ever be the "right" fit for one individual woman. We are all unique. We all have different boundaries, likes, dislikes, quirks, rules, and plans for our lives, and only a limited number of individuals will fit into our molds.

The key to discerning the difference between Mr. Right and the wrong guy is to be centered first of all in who we are. This story is about my journey to do just that. So let me start at the beginning.

My Parents

It was standard in their day, but my parents married very young—my dad was twenty and my mom was eighteen. She graduated from high school just two weeks before their wedding. Together they started a family, and although they didn't have a lot of money, they did their best with what they had. My sister and I came along a couple of years into the marriage; we were only thirteen months apart.

My dad worked as a union pipe fitter, a job that often included a lot of overtime, and my mom tended to most of the household duties. My dad proudly designed and built his vision of a dream home for his family in Minooka, Illinois, a suburb of Chicago. For him, it wasn't only "a place to hang his hat," as he likes to say, but a dream realized. In many ways, we represented a conventional Midwestern family.

Both of my parents were raised in church, but they had different religious beliefs. My mom was raised Presbyterian and my dad was raised Lutheran. After researching several religions and attending a number of churches, they eventually chose the path of nondenominational Christianity. God and the church became their foundation. They prayed about everything and turned to God for His answers to most circumstances in their lives. The church we attended was in downtown Chicago about an hour away. There were times when we attended three services a week.

From an outsiders' perspective, my childhood seemed like a very typical one. Only those who knew our family intimately had any idea that we weren't what most would consider the norm.

My Education

For a couple of years during our grade school years, my sister and I attended "video school." If you've never heard of this type of schooling, you are among the majority. Video school is a remote learning program that creates a virtual classroom for Christian schools, grades K4 through 12. Each student is supplied with a desk, a television monitor, headphones, a DVD player, and DVDs of the required classes for the year. Students watch teachers who instruct remotely in their own classrooms. Back in the day when my sister and I were in classes, we watched VHS tapes on a VCR.

My sister and I attended this program through our church, which was fairly small, so some classes had only one student and others had as many as three. It was ironic to be at school in downtown Chicago with a student body population of thirteen.

As if this scenario wasn't strange enough for us, my mom was the principal for a couple years. Was there ever a time in your childhood when you felt you knew more than your parents, but had absolutely no control over their decisions? Video school was one of those times for me.

My Morals and Openness to Equality

Our church taught us that worldly things (such as gambling, drinking, swearing, and secular music) were not right. My sister and I were limited to watching specific,

mostly Christian-based programming on TV and listening only to Christian music. We had fairly strict rules
in the house about how to treat others—to be kind and
moral, for instance. There were several years on and off
when we didn't own a TV because it became too much
of a distraction from other things we could be doing
that were more productive.

We were raised with a high set of moral values: to
respect elders, to treat everyone equally, and to honor
God. We were also exposed to different cultures and
ways of life that helped us view the world a little differently. The church we attended was 80 percent African
American, 15 percent Caucasian, and 5 percent other.
We learned that people of color weren't different from
us and that we were all created equal.

We embraced individuals from our church as family
and never let their background, status, or color define
our outlook about who they were. It's one thing to be
taught that everyone is equal, but it's entirely different
to experience personally what it feels like to be in the
minority. We were taught to accept those who were
different, regardless of the difference.

Because we moved often and changed schools,
sometimes midyear, we never belonged to any cliques
in school or had deep-rooted friendships. We had the
opportunity to enjoy suburban life, city life, and something in between. We were well rounded and had loving
parents who did their best to give us a good life.

My Foundation

My parents believed in my sister and me and taught us that we could do anything we set our minds to. They pushed us to do well in school and get good grades, but more than that, they taught us that we could realize our dreams. We were blessed, and I believe that our view of the world is different because of the life experiences we had growing up, the transitions that came with frequent moving, the people we were exposed to, and the love and support we received from our parents.

When I was nineteen, my parents divorced. Things changed significantly for me.

The divorce rocked my foundation and destroyed my trust in a lot of my relationships. It also depleted my trust in God, but it took me a long time to make this connection. Realizing that I didn't trust God when He was the core of my foundation was a very difficult thing to accept. My desire to have a family of my own was shattered by the realization that a happy marriage wasn't guaranteed and divorce was always a possibility. I realized that relationships require the commitment of two individuals and if either one decides to give up, the other cannot successfully carry the relationship on their own.

Although many kids have gone through divorce, this affected me differently because my dream from a young age was to have a family of my own. I was at an age where I was close to making that dream a reality when the divorce happened, and I didn't know where to aim my focus. Within an instant, my perspective of what my life should be had vanished and I was lost. My purpose was gone. This is when I started to meet a lot of wrong guys.

My Mistakes

During this time I didn't have the insight to separate myself from the wrong guys and only allow the right guys in. I strayed from my desire to be good, and I started to live life like it didn't matter whether I lived or died. I became too adventurous. I liked the bad-boy type of guys who rode motorcycles too fast and had too many tattoos. I spent money like it grew on trees. I dated married men. In fact, for a period of time, I dated only married men because I knew they could never commit to a relationship with me, and I never had to worry about them lying to me about what they could offer. In a sick sort of way, it was a safety net that kept me from being hurt in relationships. I drank excessively and at times would drink and drive. I was not in a healthy place.

Wrong Guy Experience

At twenty-three years old, I decided to move to California. It was a decision I will never regret, but the experience tested me in a way that almost made me give up on life.

Growing up in the Midwest, we had to contend with brutally cold and snowy winters, so a strong motivator for the move was warm weather. This was prompted by a couple of trips to Cancun that led me to believe a climate with warmer weather would make life easier and more enjoyable. It was definitely more enjoyable for a period of time, but easier was not what I experienced.

I decided San Diego was the right fit for my new life, and after securing a part-time job, I packed up all of my belongings and headed west. It was a bold move at twenty-three, but my independence wouldn't allow me to miss an opportunity that I might never have again.

My part-time job was at a restaurant, and I met a guy from Iowa who worked there. We hit it off right away. I don't know if it was his Midwestern values, his carefree personality, or his sense of humor, but I really enjoyed hanging out with him. He called me every day, he wanted to hang out every day, and he entrusted a lot of personal information with me. Even though he had his own place, he slept over at my place almost every day (but he slept on the couch).

At that point, I didn't really care to define our relationship; I was just happy to have someone who wanted to spend a lot of time with me. Had I known then what I know now, I would have never journeyed down this path. Some girls can handle a "friends with benefits" relationship, but I am certainly not one of them.

My weakness at the time was the insecure belief that no guy valued me enough to commit to me, but I felt that way because I had only dated guys who couldn't or wouldn't commit. I never allowed the single guys to get close enough. I was still fighting in every way I could to avoid disappointment. I was insecure, and I didn't care enough about myself to set standards in my relationships that could have prevented me from getting hurt. I didn't demand everything I knew I deserved and ended up settling for less than I really wanted. It worked for a while, but it wasn't satisfying my desire to have a real relationship.

Within a year of the time our relationship began, this wrong guy started taking the liberty of pursuing other girls in front of me. In his defense, he likely gave us that "friends with benefits" label, so why would I care if he wanted to be with other people? I didn't have an argument, but I also wasn't willing to allow him to date other girls while we were in a relationship. I had a conversation with him and told him I needed to set some boundaries. We could either date and be committed to each other or we could be friends and he could date other girls, but the benefits would no longer be a part of the scenario.

For a brief period of time he tried to make our relationship official as boyfriend and girlfriend, but he wasn't really ready to commit to one person so we adjusted our relationship to just friends. This worked for several months, but it was difficult for me. I did my best to enjoy the friendship, but it wasn't the same. I wanted more and he wasn't willing to give it.

That relationship played a big part in my decision to move back to Chicago, but it wasn't the only factor. I didn't really like my job, real estate was too expensive for me to buy my own place, and even though the weather was amazing, I missed my family and being surrounded by Midwestern people. California just didn't satisfy me like Chicago had. I have always had a heart for Chicago and I missed the city, its people, and the Midwestern values I grew up with and had grown to love.

When I decided to move back to Chicago, my guy friend wasn't happy at all. He wanted me to stay, but I told him that for a variety of reasons it was the right time for me to head home. It was not an easy decision and the drive home was very emotional. For almost two years, I had spent every day with him. I had grown emotionally attached and had given him my heart.

Good and Bad Compromise

Although I was willing to walk away from an unbalanced and unhealthy situation, I made too many excuses throughout the relationship and it eventually led to a very bad outcome for both of us. Six weeks after I moved back to Chicago, I had to go back to Los Angeles (LA) for my sister's wedding. I had asked my guy friend to keep some of my stuff and furniture because it saved me storage fees for six weeks. The plan was for me to fly to San Diego for the weekend, have a moving company pick up my belongings on Monday to move them back to Chicago, and then head up to my sister's house in LA for the week to attend the wedding festivities.

My guy friend and I had stayed in touch often; we talked almost every day. I was grateful that we were able to maintain such a close friendship even though our dating relationship hadn't worked out. We had become very close and shared a great deal of personal information with each other over the two years we were together. I felt secure in our relationship because we hadn't started out as boyfriend and girlfriend, but as friends. I thought that foundation protected me from being hurt, and I had let down my guard completely with him. Unfortunately, this was a lesson I had to learn the hard way.

The day I was to fly to San Diego I received a phone call from him. He said he had something to tell me but didn't want to say it over the phone. I encouraged him to tell me and explained that I could handle the truth no matter how hard it was for him to say. But he insisted we talk in person. When I got to the airport he was there to meet me and we headed back to his place. We ordered some food and had a few drinks, and he proceeded to tell me that he had met a girl two weeks before and wanted the three of us to hang out together over the weekend.

I was devastated. He knew part of the reason I had left San Diego was because it was hard for me to watch him date other girls. I couldn't understand how his two-week dating relationship was more important than our two-year friendship. I felt overwhelmed. I was so disappointed that I had put my trust in him and allowed myself to get hurt again.

I felt a deeper hurt from him than anyone I had

previously dated because I had convinced myself that friends would never turn their backs on each other. Had he told me this before I got on the plane, I would have made arrangements for him to meet the movers and for me to head directly to LA. Unfortunately, I didn't have that opportunity.

The evening went from bad to worse and he decided that he was going to head over to his girlfriend's place for the weekend. He made several attempts to call her and every time I made sure I was in the same room listening, so I knew exactly what was going on. After a few too many drinks I pulled the phone cord out of the wall several times to interrupt their conversation.

I was so angry and hurt by his actions that I flipped out and started reacting in a way that was not characteristic of me. It's embarrassing to admit now, but I was only twenty-three years old and my actions were immature and hurtful. At some point, he got tired of me shadowing him and pushed me. I fell backward and hit my head on the pedal of his bicycle. I didn't realize it at the time but it put a decent-sized gash in my head. I also didn't realize that he had called the police.

Looking back I think it's amusing that he called the police to rescue him from me, but there was absolutely nothing amusing about the situation at the time. I was heartbroken. I was angry. I was deeply hurt and felt a pain that was too much to bear. When the police arrived they "protected" him for the time it took to put a bag together and leave. They tried to settle me down, but I was crying uncontrollably.

When they left, I felt like I was at the lowest place in my life. Emotionally I felt like I had been sucked underwater and was trapped in an undercurrent, repeatedly tossed in different directions. I felt like I couldn't breathe. I was alone, out of control, and hopeless. I decided that I would never allow anyone to hurt me again.

I turned the deadbolt on the door to keep it from locking, headed down to the convenience store in the building, and purchased eight different medications that shouldn't be mixed together and a six-pack of beer. I headed back to the apartment, locked the door, put the bag on the living room table, and sat on the couch. I stared at the bag for a period of time. I don't really remember how long, but I think I was searching for any part of me that might have an inkling of hope to grasp on to. I couldn't find it.

I decided to call my mom, and I'm still not sure why. It may have been a last-ditch effort to find hope. It may have been because I wanted her to know that I was no longer going to be with her. Or it may have been that I just wanted to hear the voice of someone who cared. I knew deep down that I could get over the hurt because I had learned that emotions heal over time. But I also thought that continuing to live meant living a life closed off from all opportunities for love, or even worse—opening the door to being hurt again.

I had made the decision to never allow anyone to put me in this place again. It hurt too much. I was convinced that I would never find a guy who wouldn't hurt me. When we connect our lives with others, we obligate ourselves to consider their choices and their will, and we risk being hurt.

As you can imagine, my mom was distraught when I called her and expressed my hurt, my frustration, and my plan to end my life. She immediately called the police and asked them to head over to me ASAP. The entire time she tried to keep me on the line and did everything in her power to stop me from taking any medication. I can only imagine how helpless she felt at the time, and I've apologized to her for ever putting her though that awful experience.

I don't know what stopped me from taking the medication right away, but the police arrived within a short period of time and kept me from ending my life. While the officers were questioning me, I felt something on the back of my head and when I touched it, I realized I was bleeding. The blood running down my fingers only enhanced the pain and the crushing blows that my heart was feeling. The officers decided to take me to the emergency room.

I don't remember much of the drive there. I just felt empty and dead inside. After my mom hung up with the police, she called my aunt who lived in LA and told her the situation. She and my grandma immediately headed to San Diego. At the hospital, the doctor decided that I needed to have the wound stapled, but they couldn't give me any pain meds because I had been drinking. One of the officers allowed me to hold his hand while they stapled the wound.

There was something about this officer. I can't describe exactly what it was, but I believe he was an angel sent from above to help me get through a time I could not handle on my own. He was concerned and he cared. I couldn't figure out why this stranger cared more about me than someone who was supposed to be my friend. I'll never forget him or what he did for me. Looking back, I believe God intervened several times that day to stop me from doing something that I wouldn't have the chance to regret.

The officers stayed with me until my aunt and grandma arrived. My aunt wanted me to head back to LA that night, but I had to wait until the movers came to pick up my belongings and furniture. My grandma decided she wasn't going back to LA without me so she stayed with me the entire weekend in that apartment, being the rock that I needed to lean on.

I know if she had not been there with me holding my hand, brushing away my tears, and showing me unconditional love, I would not have survived that weekend alone. I was too frail and fragile, hopeless ... and the loneliness in that apartment would have gotten the best of me. I'm grateful for her willingness to sacrifice in a way above and beyond what most would care to do. I've expressed my gratitude to her many times since the nightmare I experienced that weekend. The movers came and packed up my belongings and furniture, and my grandma and I headed to LA. My guy "friend" didn't come back to his apartment until I was gone. My sister's wedding was a blur. I don't remember a lot of it. I drank a lot to get through it and felt sorry for my sister because I was convinced that one day her husband would hurt her and the joy of her marriage would end. I've expressed my apologies to her for not being the sister I should have been at her wedding, one of the happiest times in her life.

Had it not been for my best friend, Lori, driving cross country with me, I may not have had the motivation to get back home to Chicago. One thing I've always been proud of is my decision to not blow off my girlfriends when I am in a relationship with a guy. This decision paid off because in my time of need, I had my best friend right by my side.

Rebuilding

When I arrived back in Chicago, my life was on autopilot. I got up, got ready, and went to work every day but I didn't feel anything. I didn't care what I looked like, what I ate, or what people thought of me. I had no purpose, no goals, and no ambition. My heart was sealed by a thousand walls and I had made up my mind that nobody would pull those walls down again.

Lori and I became roommates, and for a couple

years I had the opportunity to experience firsthand her innocence, appreciation for life, and sentimental personality, which helped me find a way to put trust in family and friends again. It took much longer for me to be able to trust any guy. I also regained my trust in God and He definitely helped me find a purpose in life again and a reason to live. I realized that God puts people in your life in times of need to fill gaps and voids and help you manage difficulty. They may not always be the people you expect to fill the position, but they're always the right ones.

I believe that God intervened to make me want to put my life back together and care again about myself and the possibility of all I could accomplish in my life. This book is about how I crashed and then turned my life around.

My Insights

While some of my relationships and experiences were very challenging, I survived and I have thrived by learning from each of those painful experiences.

Getting here took me on a journey I did not expect. My frustrating and disappointing experiences led me to finally stop focusing on the wrong guys or on how some had hurt me. I began to look in the mirror and figure out what I could do to stop falling for them. A key part of the problem was not the wrong guys—it was me. In my fear of losing them, I kept losing myself. Their charming ways consistently led me to set aside my self-esteem, my well-being, and my pursuit of what was important to me.

The path I chose allowed me to find ways to free myself of the wrong guys. And the key was to understand my self-worth. My journey includes: the traps I fell into, the tears in my heart, the impact on my self-esteem, and the steps I took to break the cycle and end up happy and content, whether I have found Mr. Right or not.

This book is about sharing with you, my girlfriends, and in turn, your girlfriends what I learned and to offer practical tips to help you either avoid the mistakes I made or get out of them sooner rather than later.

Today I am successful career woman with a degree in marketing, and I also invest time in my real estate business. My focus is in residential real estate and I own investment property. I have learned the importance of a healthy work/life balance, and I have been blessed to be able to excel in both areas. As I write this I am single and have healthy relationships with the men in my life. I am not dating out of desperation, but from a place of strength and discernment.

I've seen too many of my friends marry the wrong guy because they wanted to start a family at twenty- or thirty-something and he was the guy who proposed at that time. I've heard too many of them admit that they wish they had waited and listened to their own intuition, and had not overlooked those behaviors that they convinced themselves would change one day.

From observing others and through my own experiences with wrong guys, I have learned that I would rather be single and happy than in a relationship and miserable. So I continue to devote my life to forging a successful career path, to having my money work for me, and to finding the joys in life that I'm able to capture until my Mr. Right crosses my path.

I hope after reading this book you will be inspired to do the same.

The most cruel
thing a guy can
do is make a girl
fall for him with
no intention of
catching her.

2

A Guide to Wrong Guys

S o far in this book you have met some of the wrong guys I have encountered. In listening to stories from other women, I have learned that there are some typical wrong guy patterns that appear again and again. So to help you identify those patterns, this chapter presents a guide to a wide variety of wrong guys.

Abuser (Verbal/Emotional/Physical)

Feels empowered to abuse his woman; oftentimes stems from someone else abusing him (similar to Controller and can cross over with Insecure/Fighter)

Addict

Addicted to something (gambling, drugs, porn, liquor, food, money) and is usually not capable of valuing his woman above his addiction

Aggressor

Always trying to start something with others; enjoys creating drama; likely has anger issues (similar to Fighter)

Arrogant Guy

Thinks he's better than everyone; can be demeaning to his woman

Baller

Uses his power, influence, and money to attract his woman

Cheap Guy

Cuts corners everywhere possible to save money; willing to do anything to save a dime even if it means paying more in the long run

Chronic Cheater

Can't be faithful; always looking for a woman who may be better than his

Confirmed Bachelor

Refuses to commit to anyone and would never consider marriage an option

Controller

Wants to control his woman, whether through money or power or by physically dominating her

Cougar Seeker

Seeks out an older woman solely for the experienced sex she can offer him

Emotionally Unstable Guy

Not mature enough to handle relationships; is not whole and typically doesn't love himself

Fighter

Starts fights with everyone (even his woman); always makes his woman think she's in the wrong

Gold Digger

Seeks out his woman solely for the wealth she has to offer him

Gym Guy
Attracts his woman solely with his physique; typically more interested in the way his body looks than in how his woman feels

Hot Guy
Attracts his woman solely with his looks; typically very superficial and way more into himself than his woman

Inconsiderate Guy
Never stops to think about his woman's feelings above his own

Insecure Guy
Lacks security within himself so belittles his woman to make himself feel better; makes his woman feel like she never gives him enough attention, credit, or respect

Irresponsible Guy
Wants everyone to do everything for him; asks his woman to do a lot of things he's capable of doing but doesn't care to help with

Lazy Guy
Refuses to work or do anything around the house

Liar

Lies about everything; believes his own lies; embellishes the truth to make him look better

Lover

Tells his woman he loves her within a week or two; needs to be loved so much that he doesn't understand the true meaning of love and grasps on to anything that makes him feel wanted or needed

Manipulative Guy

Makes his woman think that she is nuts because he continuously lies and doesn't want her to find out the truth; uses reverse psychology to make his woman think she is wrong

Mr. Right Now

Just wants sex

Nonconfrontational Guy

Hates confrontation so hides things and avoids conflict at all costs; always willing to agree with his woman and never stands up for what he believes in

Rebound Guy

Uses women to get over his ex

Rule Breaker
Never sticks to his own rules, much less his woman's rules; always looking for ways to get around having to do things the right way

Self-Destructor
Fears responsibility; every time he gets ahead he does something to screw things up out of fear of having to be responsible to himself or anyone else

Selfish Guy
Everything is always about him

Sugar Daddy
Thinks his woman should do whatever he wants her to if he's paying her the right amount of money

Talker
Can sell ice to an Eskimo; tells his woman stories and embellishes everything to make himself look better (similar to Liar)

Unmotivated Guy
Procrastinates on everything; makes his woman ask repeatedly to get simple things done

Unpredictable Guy
Always keeps his woman guessing so she never knows what to expect in different situations

Unreliable Guy

Never keeps his word and makes promises he doesn't deliver; hard to make plans with him or rely on him to show up when he says he will

Workaholic

Puts work above everything else

This list is not all inclusive, but provides a resource to help you identify potential wrong guys in your life. Read on for anecdotes, advice, and assignments to help you successfully lose the wrong guy—or never allow him into your life in the first place.

3

Draw a Picture of Yourself ... and Include Some Touch-ups

Have you ever looked in the mirror and thought you looked great? We've all had great hair days, and we know the feeling of finding that perfect outfit that fits our body just right. When we leave the house we feel like we are on top of the world. We feel confident, sexy, and ready to take on any challenge. These days are especially exciting for us when we have a girl's night planned and there's the possibility of meeting Mr. Right.

I don't know how many times you've gone to a bar and met Mr. Right, but my experiences have typically been meeting Mr. Right Now. Some girls are perfectly happy with Mr. Right Now because they aren't looking for a serious relationship—they're just looking to have fun. There's nothing wrong with this dating style if this is what you want, but if you want a serious relationship you must avoid two types of men at all cost: Mr. Right Now and the wrong guy. Unfortunately, you can't avoid meeting either, but you can make sure you don't spend any more time with them than absolutely necessary.

Mr. Right Now should be fairly recognizable to most women. He basically does everything in his power to get you back to his place ASAP. He will sometimes put in a little work to get there, but he usually doesn't have much patience if you indicate you want to take things a little slower and get to know him better.

The wrong guy is a little harder to detect because he isn't necessarily a bad guy. At first sight, he may even seem like the perfect guy or the guy you've been dreaming of all of your life. He could ask all the right questions and spend a decent amount of time getting to know you. He may even wait a couple of months before pressing for sex. Overall, he may seem to have all of the items on your checklist, and your friends and family may like him. But beware, because the wrong guy could seem like Mr. Right at first glance.

Kristi and Lucas

Kristi goes out with her girlfriends one night and meets Lucas at a local bar. He shows strong interest and they have a great conversation getting to know each other. Lucas asks a lot of questions and seems genuinely interested in her answers. After a short time, Kristi's friends are ready to leave, but before they head out, Lucas asks

Kristi for her phone number—and would she want to go out with him sometime? She gives him her number and agrees to see him again. Their first date is a hit!

As Kristi invests more time in the relationship, she convinces herself that Lucas is Mr. Right. She starts researching potential wedding venues, envisioning what her dress will look like, and thinking of baby names that suit them as a couple. Kristi decides it's time to become intimate and is excited to share her first night with Lucas. She wears a hot outfit and tempts Lucas all night with heavy flirting, and when they get back to his place the sex is amazing. She's on cloud nine! Kristi has finally met a great guy and she is officially in what she considers a solid relationship.

For the next week or two things are great. Then Kristi starts to notice that Lucas is not responding to her text messages as fast as he used to. He doesn't want to watch romantic comedies; he wants to watch action movies instead. Lucas is starting to go out with the guys a little more often and stops mentioning how pretty Kristi looks. She notices this change but it's subtle so she dismisses it and continues to work on their relationship.

As his behavior continues to change, Kristi decides to confront Lucas about not answering her texts, but he always seems to have an excuse: "I was busy at work." "I was at the gym and my phone was in the locker." "I have bad reception in that area." "I didn't get the text." She makes an effort to watch more action movies, telling herself that she can't always have things her way and

that in relationships, both people have to compromise.
When Lucas wants to go out with the guys more and
more often, Kristi lets him know how much it disap-
points her and that she'd rather have him spend more
time with her.

Kristi begins to press more and directly asks Lucas,
"Don't you think I look pretty in this outfit?"

He responds with the typical "Of course you do,
babe."

She continues to push: "I just had my hair done.
You didn't even notice."

He says, "I did notice. You didn't give me a chance
to say something. I think your hair looks great, like it
always does."

Even though there are some small things wrong
with her relationship, Kristi doesn't want to throw it
all away because, she tells herself, she has a pretty good
guy. He's not cheating and he's usually considerate of
her feelings, plus she has a fun time with Lucas and he
makes her laugh.

Many guys fall into this category. They put their best
foot forward initially and do almost everything their
woman wants. They know that if they can put in the
time and effort, they will get their desired reward, which
is sex. I've seen some men wait as long as six months

and jump through hoops to have sex with a woman they are very attracted to.

Men like the challenge of winning over a woman and conquering her physically. The difference between Mr. Right and a wrong guy is that when the wrong guy conquers his goal, it's difficult for him to remain interested, and his efforts to be Mr. Right quickly diminish.

Fortunately for those of us who are willing to wait for Mr. Right, we will find that he wants to establish a relationship with his woman and share his life with her. He does put his best foot forward in the beginning, but doesn't lose interest after sex because he's interested in his woman on a deeper level. He truly cares about her feelings and wants to protect her and provide for her. Ultimately, if he thinks she is his Mrs. Right, he will ask his woman to marry him.

Wrong Guy Experience

One of my encounters with the wrong guy happened when a new attorney joined the law firm where I had been working for about six years. At the time, he was dating another girl so I didn't pay much attention to him. Plus I'm a firm believer that guys should always initiate the first move. I know it's old school and traditional, but it's a requirement for any relationship I engage in. After a while, he ended his relationship with his girlfriend and began to pursue me.

Prior to my gaining an understanding of how to

successfully lose the wrong guy, I was susceptible to any guy who pursued me with abandon. It made me feel wanted, desired, beautiful, and attractive. The problem with this approach was that it made it very difficult for me to clearly see the guy who was doing the pursuing. All of the attention felt so good that it blinded me to reality. It's possible Mr. Right will pursue heavily because he's found a woman he's interested in and wants to ensure she knows how much he values her, but when a guy pursues relentlessly it's worth investing the time to consider the reason. One of those reasons could easily be that the wrong guy is "dating up" and he knows it.

At the time, his pursuit won me over and we began dating. He had captured my attention because he was different. I think he liked being different and the attention he drew from his larger-than-life personality. He had a loud voice as well, and loved telling stories that were always filled with a lot of detail and shock value at the end. He wore plus fours, argyle socks, and a plaid hat to the golf course, and often had a cigarette hanging from his mouth while he sipped Scotch. He belonged to a country club and a private club in downtown Chicago and loved rubbing shoulders with the big boys. He didn't mind the idea of an old-school gentleman's club where only men were allowed to fraternize, drink Scotch, smoke cigars, and play squash.

He appreciated the times back in the day when people dressed up for occasions. He was also down-to-earth, very smart, extremely reliable, and always engaging in conversation. His intellectual stamina and emotional vulnerability attracted me more than his physical appearance or that feeling of chemistry that can be so strong and addictive.

I knew his beat was to a different drum when he wore his golf outfit (costume) to the law firm on Halloween. I'm not sure if he was playing golf later that day, but he was the only one who dressed up, and I'm certain he loved the attention. He also loved music. He played the vibraphone and loved classical music and jazz. We went to the symphony, jazz clubs, and a variety of live music joints in the city. He was a little abrasive, sometimes cut in front of people in line or on the road, and didn't always treat the wait staff with the level of respect I would, but I wrote it off. I knew there were issues, but I didn't think they were big enough for me to break up with him. After all, none of us is perfect, and I have a lot of flaws of my own.

We dated for a year before he proposed. There were things about him that weren't exactly what I wanted in a husband, but I convinced myself that there was more good than bad, and I hoped that some of the things that turned me off would change over time. Note: this *never* happens. Any small thing that bothers you about your guy will magnify over time, especially in marriage. But part of me was happy to overlook these tiny red flags because I was so excited to be planning a wedding for the first time in my life.

He was Jewish and I am Christian. We knew that

religion could be a barrier but agreed that we could figure out a compromise to make the marriage work. We had many heartfelt discussions about how we would raise our children. We laughed at times about how ironic it would be if we ever made the decision to end the relationship because of our religious differences. Neither of us were focusing on our religions at the time and it seemed insignificant. We reached a decision that we would teach our children both of our religions and ultimately let them decide their own preference when they got older.

Although it's not consistent with my Christian upbringing, I moved in with my fiancé when I had the ring on my finger. This did not make my parents happy, and I got an earful from both of my grandmothers when they found out. I knew they had my best interest at heart so I respectfully listened, but I had decided to move ahead in this direction regardless.

Money wasn't a factor at the time. He did make significantly more than I did, but I didn't look at the relationship as one where he would be my provider. I saw us as a team, and I knew my potential would level us out at some point in the future. Shortly after I moved in, he changed. I will admit that living with him 24/7 magnified some of those characteristics that, earlier in the relationship, I did my best to ignore. But the most important thing I realized was that he was not willing to compromise very much.

He wasn't willing to change the furnishings in his

house to blend our tastes, and he started talking about my duties and his duties as if they were separate, not shared. He wasn't sharing all of his life with me, but partitioning off the parts he was willing to give up. He also changed his mind and said he wanted to raise his kids to be Jewish. He said they could be taught Christianity from time to time, but they needed to attend Hebrew school full time, become practicing Jews, and "know who they are."

Most people think marriage should be 50/50, but a good marriage should start with both individuals being whole (100/100). If you expect someone else to complete you or fill voids, you aren't fully prepared for marriage. It was now clear this was the wrong guy for me, and I knew that it was time for me to walk away from the relationship. I wanted a partner to team with and someone who wanted to share our lives together. Within five months of moving into his place, I moved out and into a new place of my own. At thirty-two, I was single once again.

In order to be successful in relationships, we must decide who we want to be, and only allow others into our lives who want to support us as that person. Compromise is necessary in every relationship, but you don't have to compromise who you are for anyone. We must set appropriate boundaries and have realistic expectations of what our life should be in order to attract Mr. Right. The only way people can take advantage of us or treat us negatively is if we allow them to.

Relationships can be great learning experiences that allow you to determine exactly what you're looking for in another person. The key is to be able to walk away better equipped and smarter and not get stuck in something that makes you settle for less than you deserve.

You can't control the actions of the people in your world, but you can control your actions and reactions. You can control who is and who isn't in your world. Our life is what it is today because of our own choices. We can't control our past, and sometimes we may not be thrilled about our current situation, but we all have the ability to control our future.

Financial Independence

One of the reasons I made the decision to get my degree was that I never wanted to rely on anyone else to support me financially. I wanted to be able to have financial freedom.

Money has always had the potential of being a huge obstacle in relationships and marriages. When each partner is not able to invest an equal financial contribution, it may become difficult for couples to decide how to spend their money.

There will always be times when financial contributions vary between partners based on circumstances in life—being a stay-at-home mom for a period of time, someone losing their job or getting a large bonus—but in general, if each side provides fairly equal value it significantly improves the financial agreement.

I also wanted to make sure that if my husband and I ever ended up getting a divorce, I wouldn't be left with whatever the courts decided was fair to give me.

Financial stability provides a woman with an enormous amount of confidence and has a significant impact on the type of guy she chooses for herself. Woman who need to rely on guys for financial security make very different decisions from those who are financially independent.

Assignment

In order to learn how to lose the wrong guy, you need to decide who you want to be ... and do whatever it takes to become that person. We all have flaws, but the important thing to remember is that your focus and efforts should be directed toward who you want to be, not who you are today or were in the past. Ask yourself these questions:

- *What are my goals?* Make the list as long as you like and include where you want to live, your desired income, the car you want to drive, your educational goals, your career path, your physical fitness and well-being, what your relationships should look like (familial, friends, and significant others), and any other criteria that come to mind that you want to achieve.

- *Who do I want to be?* This list isn't about the material things in your life that I just described, but the type of person you want to be, such as: easygoing, lighthearted, serious, open-minded, disciplined, motivated, self-aware, an overachiever, courteous to others, kind, or giving. Characteristics and beliefs define a person just as much as their goals do.

• *What do I want to look like?* Consider how you walk, talk, dress, respond to others, or solve problems. If the visual of who you are does not match what you want it to look like, consider making some changes.

You should continue to work toward being the person you want to be on a daily basis. The transition may not happen overnight, but with consistency and dedication all habits can be broken. Who you are today is not the result of luck or happenstance—it's the result of decisions you made in your past, so let your future become a result of the decisions you make today.

Motivational speakers always talk about visualizing your dream or goal and then making it a reality. It's also important to consider your environment. You can lay flower seeds on concrete and give them the precise amount of water and sunshine

they need, but flowers will not grow. Dry,
hard soil won't produce flowers either.
Flower seeds that are placed in prepared
soil with the right amount of sunshine and
water will produce flowers. You need to
make sure that the environment in which
you surround yourself is conducive to your
becoming who you want to be.

It's not what happens to you,
but how you respond to it
that matters.
—Epictetus, Greek philosopher

4

Take a Good Look in the Mirror ... Without Your Makeup On

Have you ever looked in the mirror and were scared of what you saw? We've all had bad hair days, felt self-conscious about our weight, or been ashamed of ourselves for doing something we knew was out of character for us. We're human. We make mistakes, but most of us try to get it right and be the best we can be. We can't allow failures to stand in the way of our success. We have to realize we are going to make mistakes and not be discouraged when it happens but instead pick ourselves up and start again.

One of my dear friends was in a relationship that turned abusive. At some point during her relationship she realized it was wrong to stay, but she didn't leave for more than two years. She was in a biracial marriage and didn't want it to fail. She wanted to prove to everyone around her that they were wrong about her wrong guy. She had never been involved in an abusive relationship before her marriage, and she didn't realize that things could go from bad to worse. It took a very serious event to make her realize that her life was in jeopardy.

She had struggled with self-esteem issues and felt like she wasn't good enough, pretty enough, or slim enough. She thought that if she were more perfect the abuse wouldn't be happening to her. But the moment that he pulled a gun out, she knew it wasn't her fault and she left immediately following that incident.

She never looked back. Because of her experience with that wrong guy, she built walls to protect herself from future abusive relationships. She knew she would never tolerate dating any other guy who was physically or psychologically violent. For several years after that relationship ended, she had an overly touchy trigger in her relationships because she was being overprotective. She realized the importance of protecting herself, but she took it to extremes. She did everything in her power to ensure she only involved herself with men she knew would never raise their hand to her or harm her. Her trust had been broken, and she wasn't ready to allow anyone else to do the same thing to her that her ex-husband had done.

Jennifer and Patrick

Jennifer met Patrick after she and her husband of many years got divorced. She wasn't necessarily looking for a relationship. She had been alone before and it wasn't difficult for her, but when Patrick came along he won her over with his exciting and charismatic style. His clothes were conservative yet cool—a Brooks Brothers type of guy. He wore penny loafers and an artist's beret. He wasn't that good looking and he was short, but something drew Jennifer to him. He had been a director at a Chicago dance center for a while, and he loved the arts. He worked with the Boys Club and a large charitable organization. He had also worked with a prevention program that targeted gang involvement. He could hold his own and have conversations with anyone from the president to gangbangers. Without effort, he could discuss politics, education, and current events and rub shoulders with the rich and the poor. People were mesmerized when he spoke.

Even though their relationship was like a roller coaster at times, the highs were almost equivalent to the lows. She had never cried so much in a relationship, but Patrick made her laugh just as often. They had similar personalities and enjoyed the simple things together—sometimes just sitting at an amusement park, people-watching and joking about all the things they saw. Patrick also surprised Jennifer with things that the average guy might not think to do. One time he flew Jennifer to New York for her birthday. He told her she didn't need to pack a bag because he had taken care of everything. While they were in New York they went to Tavern on the Green and the Guggenheim Museum and took a carriage ride, all in one day. They flew back the same day because Patrick had planned a surprise birthday party for Jennifer at the restaurant where she worked. To her surprise, Patrick had gotten in touch with all of her ex-boyfriends and asked them to attend the party. She believed he was trying to send the message that he had her and her exes no longer did. Patrick didn't even stay for the party himself. He left after a brief visit and then came and picked her up after it was over.

Patrick did drugs, but nobody would ever know. It had started out socially and then escalated. He was an executive director for a well-known charitable organization and did many speaking engagements for them, but at home he snorted cocaine and smoked weed. He and his father used to get high together so it was a generational thing.

Jennifer later learned that Patrick was a sociopath. He became very selfish and everything was about him. Every part of their relationship led to his self-fulfillment. He would do things that appeared wonderful and romantic, but the bottom line was to serve him. He became verbally abusive and tried to isolate Jennifer from her family and friends. He also tried to use her friends, and if he could somehow work them into his manipulative schemes, he allowed them into her life. The abuse was mainly subtle at first and Jennifer thought he was doing all of those wonderful things because he loved her and wanted to impress her.

Patrick had a purpose and a plan for everything he did. He would push to get his way and eventually, if he didn't get it, he became frustrated and the abuse escalated. The more Jennifer pushed back and tried to take a stand, the more Patrick's behavior changed from trying to impress her to trying to instill fear in her and verbally abusing her. He interrupted Jennifer as if she was a kid. He was very demeaning and often belittled her.

When it reached a point of physical abuse, Jennifer knew she had to get out of the relationship. Patrick had never punched her, but when the physical abuse reached its high he put his hands over her nose and mouth so she couldn't breathe. He also threatened her a lot, telling her that he would do things to her so nobody else would want her. He said he would throw battery acid on her at work, and assured her he could because her office was never locked and he could be gone in an instant. He said things like, "Do you think I would let you go after I've molded you the way I want you?"

Patrick's drug use worsened and he got into free-basing. He also had a sex addiction. He liked to call sex hotlines and he didn't care that Jennifer knew—he wanted her to listen to those conversations with him. He became so frustrated with Jennifer not wanting to do things his way that he pulled a gun on her. He was high on drugs at the time, and his eyes looked demonic.

Jennifer thought a woman should never have to beg a man for her life, but she did that night and it was truly the beginning of the end of her life with him. Lying in bed next to Patrick afterward, she made a promise to God. If He would get her out of this terrible relationship, she would turn her attention back to God and serve Him.

Fortunately, she was able to get out of her relationship with Patrick without missing or damaged body parts, and with her life, but she had a really hard time for a while mending from all the abuse. She was like a wounded puppy or kitten and she just wanted to be back with God. Now with the freedom to be alone, she felt peaceful and happy. God had rescued her and helped her through the days when the fear of retaliation almost overwhelmed her.

There was a volunteer at work who encouraged Jennifer by giving her a verse of scripture, a book, or a plaque. Jennifer decided she needed Christian counseling and someone who would pray with her. She found a church that was close to her apartment, and she leaned heavily on God to get her through her healing process. She had the support of family too, particularly her aunt, who offered Jennifer a place to stay and assured her that she would have peace and be safe with her there. She also told Jennifer that if her ex showed up, she would be ready for him; her aunt always kept a couple of guns close by. But Jennifer knew God was ultimately the one protecting her.

Once Jennifer knew she was rid of Patrick for good, she promised herself that she would never be with any man who might physically abuse her. Her mother had been physically abused and she never wanted to accept that into her life. But she hadn't realized she was being verbally and emotionally abused — she didn't think demeaning talk and belittling words could be abuse because they weren't physical. She had been exposed to so much violence front and center in her life, and that's what impacted her the most. When Jennifer's stepfather called her mom "crazy," for instance, it never compared to him punching her and knocking her out. The physical act seemed so much worse. It took Jennifer a while to realize that it's all abuse!

Samantha and Victor

Samantha's first marriage lasted four and a half years. She got pregnant two months after getting married and she tried to make it work, but for all the wrong reasons. Victor was seldom around and when he was he was abusive. It was mostly verbal, but it still wasn't the marriage Samantha had hoped for, and she was desperate to leave. It was her doctor who ultimately convinced her to end her marriage. She had been experiencing a lot of stress and had started to get migraines. She was under a lot of pressure to take care of her daughter and work full time. She didn't have any help from Victor; he literally was never home. He made a lot of different excuses. Samantha knew something was up but she didn't know what.

Her migraines landed her in the hospital for two weeks. The doctors had prescribed medication, but nothing seemed to help. They tried nerve blocks, which helped for a while but didn't last. She continued trying to work on her marriage, but it was difficult since she constantly struggled with headaches and never felt 100 percent healthy. Also, she really didn't want to move back home, and she didn't have enough money to support herself and her daughter. She wasn't worried about leaving Victor—she wasn't in love with him. But the idea of taking on the responsibility for herself and her daughter without any help was overwhelming. If she left, she would be a single mom and ultimately alone.

She had been seeing the same doctor since the start of her headaches and one day he told her that as long as she continued to live in the situation she was in, with her marriage to Victor and all of its added stress, she would never get rid of her headaches. Two weeks later, she decided to leave. It wasn't easy because it was her first marriage, they had a child together, and she really wanted it to work. But she realized that she had done all she could and that when two people aren't working together to make the marriage successful, it can't last. She left one weekend when Victor wasn't home. He never came looking for her. She found out later that Victor had been in a relationship with another woman for three and a half years of their marriage.

Samantha was grateful to her parents for allowing her to move back home to recover from the divorce. She had been very young when she married and was fairly young at the time of her divorce. She didn't have much and wasn't financially stable, but she had her daughter and knew she had made the right decision for herself and for her daughter's future. Victor didn't attempt to see their daughter for a year following the divorce. He tried to get Samantha back a few times, but he had remarried and she wanted nothing to do with him.

Samantha and Darren

Samantha worked hard to provide for herself and her daughter. She had a good job and owned her own home. It took her a while to get back on her feet after her divorce from Victor, but her hard work paid off and she and her daughter were doing well. Samantha met Darren and they hit it off right away. She was still fairly young and didn't have the insights to qualify the men she dated, and unfortunately her second marriage lasted only three and a half months. As bad as she thought her first marriage was to Victor, it turned out that her second marriage was much worse. Darren didn't have a job or own a home, and he didn't have any pride in trying to be the man he promised he would be. When he proposed and Samantha agreed to marry him, he swore he would get a job when they got back from their honeymoon, but never did. They tried counseling for a short time, but Samantha knew going into the marriage that they would have a very hard time making it work.

Darren complained about everything. He complained about what Samantha got him for Christmas. A couple of times he had the audacity to ask for a credit card, but Samantha told him no because he didn't have a job. Samantha wondered why she had ever agreed to marry Darren, but when she considered her age and lack of experience at the time, she realized she really hadn't known any better. She hadn't learned how to say no. When Samantha was growing up she was the oldest at home and responsible for taking care of her siblings. That was one of the reasons she had married Victor: she desperately wanted to get out of her house. She wanted to move out on her own, but her parents wouldn't let her so she had to figure out another way to make it happen. Marriage seemed to be the only route.

At that time, a lot of women married for many different reasons, most of which were not because they were madly in love. Standards were different, and most women didn't have the opportunity to live on their own. They moved straight from their parents' house to the house that they and their husbands were planning to live in. With all the responsibility Samantha was given in her family household, her parents never gave her the option to say no. She had never learned that it was within her power to refuse if she disagreed with someone or didn't want to do what they wanted her to.

She and Darren had only known each other for

three or four months when he wanted to get married. She wanted to say no but she didn't know how to and she didn't want to offend him. This is a common trait among young women who haven't had the opportunity to learn how to be independent and voice their likes, dislikes, and concerns. These women haven't yet learned the valuable lesson that their well-being is the most important thing. Instead they allow their significant others to get their way in order to keep the peace and not cause issues in their relationship.

Samantha and Darren were supposed to go on vacation and he thought it would be fun if they went to Vegas to get married. On their way home, she knew the marriage wouldn't last. She almost booked a flight home rather than driving all the way back with him, but she didn't have the courage. She was both naïve and passive.

It became evident to Samantha within a short period of time that Darren had every intention of using her financially and she wasn't about to let him. She had worked too hard to establish her independence and she wasn't about to support another person, least of all her husband. On New Year's Day, Samantha told Darren to get out. She put all of his stuff in laundry bags and changed the locks. She was finished with his lies and deception.

Unfortunately for Samantha, Darren was a little bit nuts, and he tried to tarnish her reputation a few different times. He told some of their mutual friends about her sexual preferences. She knew it was his last-ditch effort to get back at her because she wasn't going to continue to support him, but it was very hurtful. The marriage cost Samantha a great deal. After a very short marriage and a long, stressful, and costly divorce, Samantha spent more than twenty thousand dollars to be free of Darren. To this day, she looks back sometimes and gets frustrated about the loss she incurred, but she knows she did the right thing.

Samantha is now happily married and very content because she knows her husband would never put her through what Darren inflicted on her. She is now at peace knowing she can trust the person she's with, especially when it comes to her marriage, and she's learned how to be much more self-reliant.

All of these women have something in common. They were in relationships with the wrong guy, but they learned from their experiences and made changes that enabled them to better recognize wrong guys. Every woman has felt ugly or not good enough at some point or has struggled with self-esteem issues. It's usually dur-ing these times when we are most vulnerable to allowing the wrong guys into our lives, but it's important to recognize that these low points don't determine our value or worth. Even though you may allow the wrong guy in from time to time, all it takes is deciding that you are no longer willing to accept being treated less than you deserve, and to then move forward without him.

When you have a true picture of who you are and what you want out of a relationship, it better equips you to be successful and puts you in the best position to lose the wrong guy and allow Mr. Right into your life. He's the one who will appreciate you and love you even when you don't have any makeup on.

Assignment

Take some time to get comfortable with who you are without any makeup on. Dove launched a "Real Beauty" no-makeup campaign over a decade ago, and Alicia Keys recently started the trend of not wearing makeup in her personal or professional life. Some other celebrities have done the same.

I'm not suggesting you follow a trend because it's popular. I'm encouraging you to be bold and step out of your comfort zone. In my twenties I was always worried that I looked fat, but I never had weight issues. In my thirties I never went any-where without makeup on, but I was the only one who noticed. In my forties, I'm finally realizing that my physical appear-ance doesn't determine my self-worth. Try the following assignments:

• Take steps to appreciate who you are without any makeup on. If you are one of those women who never leave the house before looking your best,

challenge yourself to make a quick
run to the grocery story makeup free
(even if you have to wear sunglasses).
It might surprise you that nobody
around you cares whether or not you
are wearing makeup. It's a standard
you have set for yourself because the
media tends to portray perfection, but
the truth is that nobody is perfect.

- How can you increase your self-worth
or how you value yourself? Confidence
is key to feeling good about yourself.
Think about ways you can increase
your confidence. One way may be a
physical change: losing that last ten
pounds. Another way may be an emotional change—losing the wrong guy
and all of his verbal abuse. Another
way may be a mental change, such as
learning something new.

- Focus on what you want outside of
relationships with guys. Make a list of
ten things that are important to you
that have nothing to do with guys. Do
your best to invest time in doing more
of those things.

These challenges may put you outside your comfort zone, but vulnerability can be attractive and it empowers you to become stronger in areas where you are weak.

Even though you have physical flaws, the stronger you become mentally and emotionally, the less they seem to matter.

There is no failure except in
no longer trying.
—Elbert Hubbard

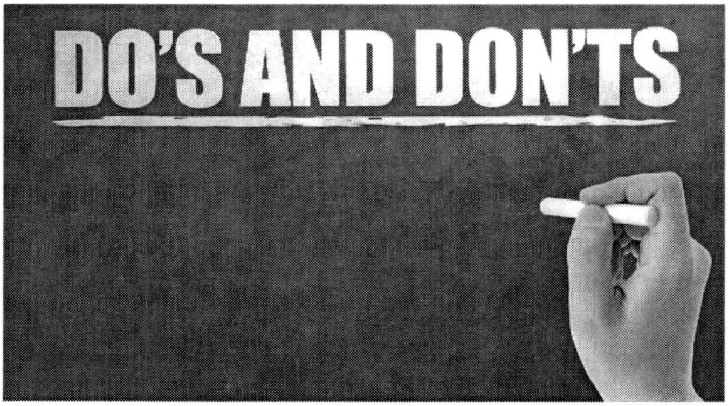
DO'S AND DON'TS

5

Consider Dating Do's and Don'ts ... But Make Your Own Rules

'm sure if you are a single woman you have come across a few lists of dating do's and don'ts. These rules seem to change based on societal norms, and can be very different depending on your culture, religion, age, or ethnicity.

In the 1920s and 1930s, women were very selective and would only accept date invitations from men with money and gifts. The dating scene among college students was very competitive and overwhelmingly populated by men, who sometimes had to fight for dates with the most desired female students. At that time, too, most women got married just as a means to move out of their parents' home.

In the 1940s and 1950s, young male adults in the

United States were scarce because of the mandatory draft implemented in World War II. Most young men were at war overseas and thousands never returned. Women became less concerned with a man's status and more with his likelihood of survival. A new relationship style called "going steady" also emerged, where men gave women an article of clothing to publicize their commitment. Most women got married very young and oftentimes married their high school sweethearts.

In the mid-1960s and 1970s, the Women's Movement became very popular, and with the emergence of the birth control pill, a sexual revolution began. This marked the end of typical dating and the beginning of the "hookup" culture. Young adults began partying and experimenting with alcohol and psychedelic drugs in large groups. The United States Supreme Court's *Roe v. Wade* case legalized abortion nationwide. This changed a lot of women's perspective about the level of control they had over their own bodies.

In the 1980s and 1990s, matchmaking services became a great way to meet people, and going on blind dates was acceptable. The threat of STDs became prevalent, so a lot more caution was taken before casually having sex. Men knew the three-day rule that required them to wait that long before calling women for a second date, and women actually waited for the call and were excited when the phone rang. A woman knew a guy was head over heels for her when he made her a mix tape. Women were no longer pressured to get married and have kids by the time they reached their mid-twenties.

Today, the dating rules have completely changed. Women meet men online more often than they do in person, and texting has become the easiest way to communicate, so phone calls are almost nonexistent. Our modern-day society has also introduced the world of dating apps so the options of finding potential men seem limitless, geographical barriers are obsolete, and women have a hard time "settling" down because they fear they might be missing the next best thing. Although apps have made finding a potential date for the evening as easy as swiping right, there is a lot more competition because of the seemingly endless options. A benefit to dating apps and social media is that women can get to know a lot about a potential guy by investigating him online, without him ever knowing. It's not uncommon for women to wait until their late thirties or early forties to get married and have kids. They want to have their independence before settling down.

Priscilla's Rules

Priscilla hasn't had many relationships, but that's been by design. She's at a stage in her life when it's not her highest priority, so she doesn't spend a lot of time seeking men to date. She didn't date many men before she was married either, and later realized that had been one big mistake. But her dad was very strict, and it didn't seem worth the argument she had to have with him in order to get permission. She started dating her husband when she was eighteen, and five years later they married.

Today, Priscilla is divorced. She will explore a relationship with someone if it seems worthwhile, but she's got so many other things filling up her time that it's not something she pursues. She evaluates potential men by their physicality, profession, confidence, and sense of humor. She also requires them to be dependable and articulate, and show leadership qualities. They need to be aware of their surroundings when out in public spaces, and they need to have the acumen to adjust to social situations. She prefers men who value their physical, emotional, and spiritual well-being and have a sense of family. It's also important to her that they are tall and have hair. This may seem superficial to some women, but to Priscilla attraction and chemistry play a significant role in successful relationships.

Priscilla qualifies the men she considers dating by spending a decent amount of time with them before getting into a relationship. She wouldn't start dating someone she had just met at a bar. There have to be synergies. She takes the time to get to know them as friends first, through conversation, storytelling, and personal experiences. She ensures that she knows them well before she gets emotionally involved.

She's also done some online dating, which required a completely different vetting process: she would have to ask those qualifying questions electronically. Then she would meet the guys and continue the query in person. She's been told by several men that she asks too many questions, but she hasn't changed her strategy because those guys need to be qualified to date her or it's not worth her time. She has considered that she may need to soften or disguise the questions better, but somehow she needs those questions answered or she's not moving forward with any guy.

Nancy's Rules

Nancy is currently single, but she's had four meaningful, long-term relationships. At the time she was involved with these guys, she thought the relationships were great. Three of them happened during a time when she did not have a relationship with God so her mind-set and priorities were different. When all of these relationships started, she thought she would marry the guy she was dating.

Nancy now qualifies any potential guys she dates. One of her qualifiers is that the guy has to believe in God. In fact, it's her only nonnegotiable quality. She doesn't have many limits as far as race or ethnicity goes because she's attracted to all of them. She appreciates and honors the idea that God created everyone equally, and although she may not be familiar with all cultures she's open to learning about them. Another qualifier for her is that the guy has to be honest and have integrity. He can't just talk the talk ... he has to walk the walk. Nancy tries to observe the guy's character and how he interacts with other Christians, as well as whether he has a sense of humor. He doesn't have to have the same sense of humor as she does, but they need to be compatible. She wants someone to get her jokes, not someone who would take her wrong if she says something sarcastic or witty. She also thinks it's important that both people understand each other. Nancy shared that it has taken time to learn how to qualify potential guys but the effort has paid off.

Nancy and a friend served at church together and even though he transferred to another campus, they kept in touch. They had experienced similar losses; she lost her grandparents, who were very close to her, and he understood that type of loss so they developed that connection. They weren't interested in dating each other, but they maintained a friendship.

Then Nancy met one of his friends and was very interested in him. She asked her friend about this potential guy, and he told her his friend had been really supportive of him, had in fact helped him through a time of depression and paid for his counseling sessions. That showed Nancy what type of character this potential guy had, which revealed a lot about his integrity and character. She's also observed potential guys who see someone struggling and help them or do other acts of service by helping others, and it tells her a lot about their motives and what's in their heart. It shows that they are willing to be inconvenienced in order to help others. Being thoughtful, serving others, and showing kindness are all genuine things that speak to a person's character.

Another way Nancy tries to determine whether someone is honest is by making sure they live authentically. She wants to know they believe what they say ... that they live it. Nancy doesn't necessarily have "tests," but until she goes through certain experiences with a potential guy, it's difficult for her to believe they are doing what they say and are true to their word. She also looks for good qualities displayed in their life. It's not important to her that they may go to church on Sundays; it's important what their life with coworkers, neighbors, and family looks like.

Tammy's Rules

Tammy is single and has never been engaged or married. She's dated occasionally, but she's only had two relationships that were serious enough that she would consider them long term. Tammy qualifies all potential guys, and she's learned the importance of faith and how attractive it is when a guy pursues God and can lead her in that. She's come to a place in her life where when she meets men, she's not afraid to ask about their faith or share her faith with them.

Tammy is convinced actions speak louder than words. She doesn't allow potential guys to just tell her who they are ... she has to *see* who they are. When things aren't going perfectly, she looks at how they respond to the situation. If she knows them, she also questions friends or the potential guy's friends to find out more about their background. She's learned it's something that just takes time. If the guy can show her through actions how he handles things and she's impressed with it, she's open to getting to know him better. It's also important for her to hear the guy's thought process, especially when she is getting to know him on a deeper level. When she learns why he feels a certain way, it can be very appealing to her and helps her understand the guy's character.

For Tammy, God has to be at the center of any potential guy's life and that's something she can figure out pretty easily. Her second boyfriend invited her to volunteer with him for one of their dates. He regularly volunteered at an organization and she thought it spoke highly of his character to not only volunteer, but to invite her to be a part of it. That night they were volunteering, they learned that the donations fell short of what the organization was expecting and he went out to buy more items to ensure their goal was met. That generosity made her realize that he was a great person. She looks for the same characteristics and qualities in every potential guy she dates. She doesn't want to put herself in a situation where she has to be uncomfortable or feel it's necessary to put up walls to protect herself. She doesn't want to be in any awkward situations either. She's learned enough to know she's only going to date guys who are marriage material.

Dorene's Rules

After forty years of marriage, Dorene's husband passed away. She has been a widow for seven years. She hasn't had many relationships throughout her life because she got married very young and when her husband passed, she didn't have a strong desire to start dating again—in fact, the thought of dating again kind of turned her stomach. The idea of being vulnerable and trying to put her best foot forward to ensure that a potential guy might like her seemed exhausting to her.

Dorene feels she has a pretty amazing life. She's a pastor at her church, she has two wonderful married children, and she has three of the most amazing grandkids. She's got plenty of friends for companionship, and she doesn't feel that she needs to be in a relationship to be happy. She's got some great guy friends and in some ways that fills the void of no longer having her husband in her life. She likes conversing with men and hearing them share their perspectives. Men think differently from women and Dorene loves the way they think. She likes how most men are real and just get to the point. They often don't have a lot of emotional baggage so things are sometimes more simple and clear cut from their point of view. She wouldn't say that she never wants to date again, but it would have to be the right person at the right time.

When the opportunity presents itself, Dorene qualifies all men she may consider dating by getting to know them. She has to have some familiarity with them, so they have to be friends or at least acquaintances for a while first. If the potential guy is a friend of a friend, she may be open to meeting him but only in group settings so she can get to know the guys' personality, character, integrity, and other qualities. She's at a place in her life where it's not worth dating just to be with someone, so any potential guy has to bring enough to the table to make it worth her investment.

Dorene does premarital counseling for couples in her church who want to marry, and one of the key things she tells them is that the only way to have a successful marriage is to keep their focus vertical, not horizontal. When both the husband and the wife keep their focus on God, the marriage can be successful because ultimately God is driving. However, when either the husband or the wife (or both) are looking at each other hoping that this other person can make them happy and whole, marriage becomes a very big disappointment and is likely to end up in divorce.

All four of these women have established different rules for their stages in life. You can probably relate to some but not all of the rules they have decided are most important. Have you ever asked yourself what constitutes good dating advice and what is appropriate at different stages of dating? The good news is that there isn't one set of rules across the board that applies to everyone. The rules change depending on your stage of life, and at times, it's a good idea to break the rules. In order to figure out the right set of rules for yourself (at any given stage) you must first be completely honest with yourself.

The rules you make for yourself should align with your dating goals. If you aren't looking for anything serious and you want to get out there and meet a lot of new people, then date as often and as much as you like. Don't worry about the quality of the people you date because your goal is simply to have fun.

If you are looking for something serious, your dating rules should reflect a much higher standard. The quality of guys you choose to date will be a direct result of your lifestyle going forward.

There are some good dating rules out there. Some dating do's and don'ts come into play before you actually start dating. One of my favorite dating books is Patti Stanger's *Become Your Own Matchmaker*. In it, she advises women to do a "dating detox" to make sure they are in the right state of mind to date.

I think it's important to consider where you are emotionally and whether you are ready to date. If you've been doing a lot of dating and feel like it's more work than fun, take a little time off and focus on yourself. Dating shouldn't feel like a job.

When you are ready to get back in the game, Patti also offers advice about online dating, where to meet men, and how to make your dating experience more enjoyable. One thing she advises is to make a list of things you want to do: restaurants you've always wanted to try, activities that require a date, items on your bucket list, for example. When you start dating again and a guy asks you what you want to do or where you want to eat, you've got a list handy. The icing on the cake is that even if the date doesn't go well, at least you were able to check out that trendy new restaurant you've always wanted to try, or check off a helicopter ride from your bucket list.

Some rules exist for your own protection. If you are dating to find a serious relationship, there are some very important rules you should follow to ensure that you filter out any of the wrong guys and only allow in Mr. Right. Steve Harvey refers to himself as the CLO (Chief Love Officer) and has some pretty good dating advice. One of his rules is that women should make men wait ninety days before becoming intimate. This may seem absurd to some women, but if you are looking for Mr. Right this is a great way to keep your emotions out of your decisions. When you avoid intimacy, logic and reason speak much louder and you are able to hear the right information and make more informed decisions.

Soul Ties

When I was growing up, my parents taught me about "soul ties." Simply defined, it is the tying together of two souls. These ties can be good or bad, and are typically formed when there is intimacy in a relationship.

Some examples of good soul ties include: best friends, siblings, married couples, and a relationship between a parent/child or grandparent/grandchild. Some examples of bad soul ties include: fornication (having sex outside of marriage) and an abusive relationship.

A good soul tie can be a blessing because it allows two people to have a very close connection in a special, healthy way. They can lean on each other for support, emotionally build each other's confidence or self-esteem, and help each other through difficult times.

Bad soul ties can be devastating and have detrimental effects on those in the relationship. Have you ever wondered why women who are in abusive relationships can't seem to leave? Or why that guy you slept with one time three years ago still pops into your mind from time to time? Or why you can't seem to stay away from a guy you know isn't good for you—why you feel an uncontrollable draw toward him?

These ties draw us to others in good or bad ways. When you become intimate with someone, you allow your emotional attachment to lead the way and neglect to use logic and reason. This is one reason it's important to follow certain rules that will help protect you from all of those wrong guys who surround you every day.

If you are tired of reading all of the standard dating do's and don'ts that may not apply to you, you might enjoy the perspective I share on breaking some of these rules.

Consider Breaking These Rules:

Do expect to meet men in unexpected places

I realize that everyone has heard that one story about a friend of a friend who was shopping in the grocery store in the vegetable section and met the man of her dreams, or was grabbing a cup of coffee on her way into the office and bumped into an old boyfriend from high school—and they ended up getting married. These stories are *not* common. Trust me!

I can't remember the last time I made eye contact with someone walking down the street, in a store, or on public transportation. *Everyone* is in their own world, listening to music, checking email, scrolling through Facebook, swiping left on Tinder, or playing Candy Crush. While it's a good idea to be open to meeting someone new at any time, I wouldn't go so far as to say you should expect it.

Don't be too available

I am a firm believer that men should make the first move, but I don't believe that women should make themselves unavailable just to give a guy the impression that they're not desperate. My girlfriend was sitting in church one Sunday and noticed a guy sitting in front of her who was six-feet-five. She's six-feet-three so she noticed him, but didn't pay much attention to him until after the service when he turned around and starting chatting with her.

When he asked her if she wanted to go to lunch, she had to stop and think for a moment what the right move would be. She reconsidered her initial reaction to say no, then took a second look at the situation, went with her gut, and decided to go with him. As long as the guy is taking the initiative, it's okay to be available to take his calls or go out with him at the last minute. On the other hand, if he ends up asking you out at the last minute on a consistent basis, it's time to set some boundaries.

Do be confident and make the first move

You may not agree with me on this one, but I say men *always* need to make the first move. It's true times are changing and we may not traditionally date as we did in the past, but as Patti Stanger says, "men are hunters" and "they like the chase." When we pursue men, it takes the fun out of it. They were created to pursue us. It's instinctual for men. It's part of their nature.

Some of my best dating memories are of times when I met new guys and they pursued me. It is such a self-esteem builder to have a guy approach me and start up a conversation or ask for my phone number. I take it a step further and allow the guys I date to chase me a little longer because the initial anticipation builds and there's nothing that compares to that romantic spark when his hand touches mine or that electric chemistry when we share that first kiss. Hold on to that new and exciting time as long as possible.

Don't worry about his age—or yours

While it's true that love may not be ageist, common sense should tell you that if there's a significant difference between your age and your guy's age, there will be more hurdles to overcome in your relationship. Your interests may not be the same, you may be at different places in your schooling or career, you may want to start a family at different times, and you may want to retire at different times. I personally would recommend keeping the age difference to about ten years max.

Do date outside of your faith

Most people may think it's a good idea to be open-minded when it comes to dating and mixing religion, but I think this is an area that can't be compromised. My engagement to the Jewish guy may have influenced my perspective, but I believe having the same faith as your guy can make marriage a lot easier. I'm not saying that it can't work, but like dating someone who is significantly older or younger than you, there will be a lot more hurdles to overcome.

I've met some guys who have given me a terrible first impression, but over time I grew to like them. I've also met some guys who I was not at all attracted to but after a couple months of hanging out with them as a friend, I grew more attracted to them based on their personality. I've heard of one-night stands leading to lasting relationships, so you can't always put labels on everything or expect that following dating do's and don'ts will make everything work out.

At the same time, it's probably best to play it safe and consider yourself as part of the majority where the normal standards apply. You can cling to the hope that your Mr. Right will come along riding a white horse, looking like Fabio in the romance novels and drawing his sword to defend your honor, but it's not likely.

Assignment:

Ask yourself these questions:

- Do I want a serious relationship?
- Do I want to date as many people as possible to gain dating experience?
- How much time do I want to invest in dating?
- Do I consider dating a fun way to spend my time or does it feel like a job interview?
- If I never had the opportunity to date again, how would it make me feel?

I don't think it's a bad idea to seek dating advice, but I recommend researching a lot, tapping into many resources, and using common sense about what you know works best for you. It's not necessarily a bad idea to have a list of dating do's and don'ts, but don't be afraid to break the rules sometimes when your gut is telling you that it's the right move.

The greater danger for most of
us lies not in setting our aim
too high and falling short; but
in setting our aim too low, and
achieving our mark.
—Michelangelo

6

Re-Prioritize ... Your "In Case of Emergency" Numbers

E veryone who has dated seriously or been in love has experienced disappointment and heartbreak. Nobody enjoys going through a breakup, whether it's your own choice or not, but most of us have been fortunate enough to have at least one good friend or family member to help us get through it.

I've had a fair share of disappointment, heartbreaks, and breakups ... and fortunately I've always had someone nearby to hold my hand. I think we all go through phases when we are more insecure than in others, but during those vulnerable times we should be able to turn to our loving support system to get through.

Jenna's Story

Jenna is currently divorced. She started dating her ex-husband when she was eighteen years old, and she knew he was "it" from the minute she met him. During the years they dated, and for most of their marriage, they were really good together. They goofed around a lot and both loved entertaining each other. They were the couple people flocked to because they were having so much fun—until they weren't. Her ex-husband genuinely loved her, admired her, and respected her. They were great friends and loved being together.

He was from Kansas City and she was from Chicago, so as a compromise they decided to spend five years in Kansas City and five in Chicago. Jenna is a Chicagoan through and through and her ex-husband had a business in Kansas City so it was difficult for either of them to make the compromise to move. In the end they chose Kansas City first. They got along really well, but his mother was very involved (too involved) in their relationship. She believed that her opinion was the only one that mattered and Jenna's opinion didn't matter at all. She referred to Jenna as the "no good MFer." She consistently manipulated Jenna's ex-husband to ensure that he and Jenna were at odds. She always chose him over Jenna and her family, which was hard.

Jenna bought her ex-husband a dog and one day he told Jenna it had died. Years later he confessed that he had seen the dog later at a neighbor's house. Jenna found out that his mother had sold it to their neighbor.

Jenna didn't really like the dog, but what an extreme for his mother to go to just to try to hurt her! She was very manipulative.

When the five years was up, Jenna decided it was time to go back to Chicago as they had originally agreed. She was tired of him not standing up for her, and she was done dealing with his controlling and abusive mother. Jenna worked hard to have a successful marriage, but her ex-husband never put her first. He put his mom first and didn't do anything to stop her from mistreating Jenna.

Jenna moved back to Chicago, in July, while her ex-husband tied up some loose ends with his business in Kansas City. During this time he became more and more distant. They talked occasionally but not like a married couple. By the end of February, her ex-husband had fallen off the face of the earth.

By his birthday on April 9, Jenna hadn't heard from him in weeks. She knew at that point he wasn't coming to Chicago. Jenna didn't know if he had ever really planned on moving, but it became clear to her at that point that he never would. For a long time after that, Jenna was still hopeful that he would eventually come to Chicago, but he didn't. She later found out that he got a girl pregnant, and she knew then she was no longer a factor in his life.

Jenna's parents helped her get through her divorce. They told her it was time to get out of the marriage. They told her to cut the cord because it wasn't worth it to wait for her ex-husband to come to Chicago, or to fight for the relationship any longer. Jenna's friend told her the same thing. They were very supportive. Her grandma also helped in a huge way, both financially and emotionally. Jenna and her grandmother had a connection because her grandmother had had an abusive mother-in-law too; she could empathize. In fact, she had counseled Jenna on the phone for hours when she lived in Kansas City. She loved Jenna so dearly and didn't want her youngest grandbaby to endure what she had; she wanted to help her get out of that bad relationship. She ultimately convinced Jenna that "enough is enough" and supported her to ensure she had the opportunity to leave. Jenna and her grandmother share the same soul. To this day, Jenna will say something and her parents will call her "Barbara," her grandmother's name. She gave Jenna something she never had: the choice and voice to say, "No more."

Rebecca's Story

Rebecca is currently happily married. Her worst relationship was with a guy she dated in her mid-twenties. He said all the things she wanted to hear, but she couldn't trust him. The longer she was with him, the clearer it became that he was a liar. He could talk his way out of anything. He was not always available to her, and his stories were shady.

His ex-girlfriend lived with him, and he said it was because she had crazy parents who wouldn't allow her back into their house. Rebecca believed this until one day she dropped him off at his apartment. He tried to call his ex-girlfriend over so Rebecca could meet her, but she wouldn't and she was crying. Rebecca realized that he was likely still dating this girl. He continued to lie and tried to hide it from Rebecca, but she knew that was why he was unavailable and always making excuses. He couldn't hold down a job either, which made it hard for her to know where he was consistently. He would tell Rebecca that he wanted her to meet his family, but then never scheduled a time to meet.

Rebecca got fed up at times, knowing he was lying, and told him she didn't want to be with him anymore, but he always found a way to talk her out of leaving him. He kept trying to convince her he wasn't a liar, but she knew deep down in her heart that he was and that's why none of his stories ever made sense. Rebecca stayed in the relationship longer than she should have because he was very attractive and had a great personality, and there was chemistry. He made her second-guess herself and feel like she was crazy for not believing him. Once Rebecca finally left him, she was certain that those same stories worked on a lot of girls.

Fortunately, Rebecca didn't settle for less than she deserved. She talked to one of her good friends and asked for her honest opinion. She wanted to figure out if she was really being crazy, or if he was just making her feel that way. Rebecca's friend helped her realize he was lying and she was being gullible, even though Rebecca wanted to believe everything he told her was true.

It was not easy for Rebecca to muster the courage to leave because sometimes in a relationship it's easier to deal with the negative than to try to end it and either look for another guy or end up alone. It can seem harder to move on to the next guy to see what he has to offer, which might not necessarily be better than the guy you are dating now. Breaking up means dealing with the whole dating thing again, and that can be so exhausting. Fortunately for Rebecca, she cared enough about her well-being and about doing what was best for her.

Corrine's Story

Corrine is a widow who was married twice. Many years into her second marriage, her husband died suddenly. She's been single again for more than twenty years.

Her first husband was an alcoholic who would disappear for days and weeks at a time. When he was sober, he was the nicest man but when he was drunk, he was abusive and unreliable. At every place he worked, they were crazy about him; he had a good work ethic. He was legally blind and wore very thick glasses. Every night when they walked home Corrine guided him along. He had it in him to be a very good man, but one drink and he'd be gone on a binge for weeks. Afterward, he would romance Corrine and say all the right words. Things would be good for a little bit, but then she would get pregnant and he would take off. This happened for all three of her pregnancies.

Corrine had to get government financial support to help pay for food and rent. She was a hard worker and wasn't taking advantage of the system, but she needed enough to feed her girls and keep a roof over their heads. The financial support helped but didn't cover everything, so she had to get a job at the local diner.

Even though Corrine was extremely frustrated at her ex-husband for leaving her to fend for herself and their three girls, she never would have divorced him because she didn't believe in divorce. She had been taught that it wasn't an option, but the government eventually told her she had to divorce him or they would stop giving her financial support, telling her that if he wasn't going to contribute to the system, they weren't going to help him or his family. So Corrine divorced him. He didn't contest it because he was gone, but it wasn't easy. Corrine's three girls were going to have to rely on her alone to take care of them.

After the divorce, Corrine felt more strongly that she could take care of herself. She got a job in the kitchen of a high school making salads. She liked that job; it made her feel needed. Another reason she knew the divorce was the right thing to do was for the sake of her girls. In those days most women didn't get divorced because they had no other financial means of support. Corrine told herself that she had asked for the abuse because she married the guy, but her daughters hadn't asked for it, and it wasn't fair to them, so she knew she had to leave. Once the divorce was finalized, she was happy it was over. She had finally gotten out from under her ex-husband's mess. She knew he wouldn't change and he wouldn't get better because he was an alcoholic who was in denial and wouldn't change until he admitted there was a problem.

Corrine didn't have much after the divorce, but she had her girls and made it her priority to hold their family together. She focused on God and followed His lead and, with His help, she knew they would make it — and they did. Neighbors and church friends helped along the way. Her third daughter got impetigo (a terrible skin condition) and her neighbor told her that if she accompanied her at church, God would heal her. Corrine said, "Yeah, right," but her neighbor encouraged her and took her to church. Corrine had gotten the diagnosis on Sunday and by Wednesday's church service her daughter was completely healed. That was when Corrine met her Lord. A short time later her second husband came along. He adopted her three girls, they had a fourth daughter together, and they were happily married for many years.

Sandra's Story

Sandra is currently divorced. She has been in a few relationships that were good for the most part. Her worst experience was the divorce from her ex-husband, who wouldn't take charge and share their responsibilities.

It wasn't in his DNA and she couldn't blame him for the type of person he was, but she would have come to despise him if she decided to stay married 'til death did them part. Sandra admits the divorce was a terrible thing for her to go through—very difficult for her, her family and her children—but she knew she had to or things would have ended very ugly.

Sandra knew that her family and daughters didn't understand her reasoning for the divorce. Outsiders looking in didn't get it either. Her ex-husband wasn't a bad guy. He did a lot of good things (gave her freedom, was decent, and had morals), and it made her wonder at times if divorce was the right decision. So often, though, only the two people involved in the relationship know what's going on and it's hard for anyone else to see the truth. It was devastating to Sandra to have her husband there but not have that connection. When the divorce was final, she didn't regret it. She knew it was the right thing for her to do at the time.

Sandra's divorce was a profound experience for her and she hopes to never be put in that position again. She disappointed everyone. She believed in the vows "for better or for worse," but somehow that vow needed to be realigned in her and her ex-husband's real-life situations. Unfortunately, they couldn't find that balance. Sandra felt that because she was the one who initiated the split, she had let everyone down. She thinks that in general, women allow things to go on longer than they should. She feels that women's intuition tells us when a situation's not right, but we don't listen because we are pleasers and nurturers by nature, and we just take on more than we should.

Sandra came to the realization that her mom had put up with a lot from her dad because generationally it was her role. At the time it was the cultural norm and Sandra's mother was not educated. She didn't have other resources so she stuck it out. Both of Sandra's sisters, younger and older, had gotten divorced at the same time and her mom was upset; she felt that neither one of them had put up with what she had. Her sisters didn't deal with all the stuff Sandra's mother had to deal with during her marriage. What Sandra's mother didn't see was that her daughters had choices—they didn't have to stay in it. They could handle life on their own financially and emotionally.

Unfortunately, one of Sandra's daughters doesn't have that insight yet. She would rather be with some-one than be alone, even if she realizes that the person she's with is not making her happy. It's unfortunate in Sandra's opinion, but she is hopeful her daughter will mature and become better able to qualify men before she gets into a relationship. Sandra feels that relationships should be about enhancing one another and making a positive difference in each other's lives.

Tara's Story

Tara is currently happily married. Her worst relation-ship was when she was head over heels for a guy who cheated on her during their entire relationship. She didn't find out until three years into the relationship that he had slept with everyone he could, including some of Tara's best friends. There were a lot of drugs and physical abuse involved in the relationship as well. Tara admits she felt desperate to be in love with him and stay with him. She put him on a pedestal and convinced herself that he was amazing. She wanted him to want her. She was sure that being alone would have been worse than being with him. She reached out to her dad for support, and with his help and guidance, she finally realized that the only way she would be able to leave him would be with God's help. When she reached out to God she grew strong enough to leave this guy and it ended up being pretty easy to walk away. She later realized that being alone would have been much better than being with him. Tara was fortunate enough to have a solid support system to help her get out of that relationship.

After that relationship, Tara felt very beaten down so she looked to God to help her find the right guy. She knew God had to have a bigger plan for her than her typical lifestyle during that time. She might have had more expectations at that time than she realized, but she was very young and didn't think about all of the things she would look for in a potential mate for the rest of her life. She qualified her relationships, but knew she needed God's help when it came to the guy she would marry. Some of the qualifiers for her relationships were obvious characteristics: good person, solid, not a cheater, someone who was serious and treated her the way she needed to be treated. Honesty and integrity were also very important to her. She qualified potential guys by spending time with them and meeting their family and friends.

When Tara met her husband, they dated briefly and then she met his family. He invited her to church and she accepted the invitation. That Sunday she met God. It was hard for her to worry about qualifying her husband because once she came to know God, she felt He had led her to that place and had introduced her to her husband for a reason.

She and her husband are happy, but their marriage is not perfect. There have been times when she has asked herself why she didn't look for someone who had such and such, or different qualities than her husband had. You may have heard about the "seven year itch," when married couples struggle more at certain times. Tara admits that both she and her husband have felt the same way at different times in their marriage ... that they are stuck with each other and have wondered what they are doing and how they ended up in that place together. Even though their marriage is not perfect, Tara knows that her husband is the best partner for her and she wouldn't be happier with anyone else. Marriage isn't always easy and sometimes it takes work, but the reward of having a good marriage is well worth the cost.

All of these women went through some very difficult relationships and experiences, but all had a support system or higher power to turn to for help in losing the wrong guys. Once you are strong enough to make the decision to walk away, you need to ensure that you have a solid support system around you to help you continue down that path. Enlist the help of close friends, family members, and anyone in your circle who will be willing to listen to you and have your back. When you are tempted to go back to the wrong guy, call anyone and everyone on your "in case of emergency" contact list. Talk it out as much as you need to, scream until you lose your voice, use your pillow as a punching bag until your hand hurts, cry until you have no tears left ... but whatever you do, do not go back. When you take the appropriate steps to date Mr. Right and avoid the wrong guy, you will have significantly fewer breakups and heartbreaks.

Assignment

In order to determine what type of support system you need, ask yourself these
questions:

- Am I strong enough to walk away from
  a bad relationship?
- Am I motivated enough to find a different job if the one I have is not making
  me happy?
- Am I adventurous enough to move out
  of state by myself?
- If one of my friends took up all our
  time together and never gave back,
  would I end that friendship?
- Am I a leader or a follower?

These questions may not all revolve
around dating, but answering them will
help you determine your level of strength
to make decisions that are good for you,
even if they aren't easy ones.

The time is always right
to do what is right.
—Martin Luther King, Jr.

7

Remove ... Your Rose-Colored Glasses

Have you ever made an excuse for your own behavior? I can have the extra scoop of ice cream ... I'll just workout a little longer tomorrow. I can afford that fourth pair of shoes ... I'll just put it on a credit card and pay it off next month. I can have a few too many drinks when I'm out with the girls tonight ... it's Friday night, it's been a stressful week, and I've worked hard so I deserve it.

Have you ever made an excuse for someone else's behavior? I know my boyfriend talks down to me ... but he has a lot of insecurity from the way his mother treated him growing up. I know my boyfriend calls me derogatory names ... but he doesn't know better—his father was verbally abusive to his mother. I know it was wrong for my boyfriend to hit me ... but it was just that one time and he promised it would never happen again. I know it's not right for my boyfriend to abuse me (ever in any way) ... but he's trying to get better and I'm here to help him and show him what true love really means.

An excuse is defined as "overlooking a fault or error" or "seeking to remove the blame of." What makes us want to excuse our own actions, or those of others?

Why do we find ourselves in situations where we make excuses for behavior that tears us down (or someone else)? Can we ever justify those type of excuses?

Learning from Experience

When it comes to learning the hard lessons, there are two different types of people:

- Those who like to learn from their own experience
- Those who like to learn from the experience of others

I prefer to learn from the experience of others because it's much easier and less costly. We obviously all make mistakes from time to time, but by observing others and learning from their experiences we can lessen the number of mistakes we make in our own lives.

I've learned a lot about relationships by watching friends, coworkers, colleagues, peers, and family. I've read books. I've read Facebook posts. I've observed people in public. It's interesting to see what the persona of a relationship is versus the truth of the relationship. A relationship on Facebook may seem perfect, but the truth may be that there is infidelity. The real truth of a relationship is only known by the two people who are involved in it, and only they can decide what they are or are not willing to accept.

When I was in my thirties, although I had been engaged, it didn't turn out the way I expected. I was disappointed to have to return to being single. A lot of my friends were getting married and on the path to starting a family. It wasn't easy to watch them move forward with their lives while mine seemed to be at a standstill. Yet as much as I wanted a family, I couldn't settle for something less than I deserved.

The following stories are based on true accounts. I hope they will help you learn from others so you can avoid having to go through similar experiences yourself.

Nicole's Story

My friend Nicole married in her early thirties, and although she had seen some red flags when she and her husband were dating, she wrote them off. She told herself that she wasn't perfect, no relationship would be everything she ever wanted, and everyone has to compromise about some things. They had an amazing wedding and an awesome honeymoon, and they bought a big, beautiful house in a suburban tree-lined neighborhood. She was making her dreams come true.

During the first year of marriage, both she and her husband had to make some adjustments. They were establishing boundaries and learning what the other person would and would not tolerate. The second year of marriage proved to be a little bit more difficult because he expected her to compromise more, while he was willing to compromise less. Even though she worked full time, she found herself doing all of the chores around the house and even some of the landscaping.

She found out they were expecting a baby and the focus shifted to the joys of becoming a mom. Once the baby was born, her husband made it clear that she was also expected to be the baby's primary caregiver. She loved being a mom. The whole experience was so exciting and such a joy for her. She didn't mind that her husband didn't get up at night when the baby cried or volunteer to change dirty diapers, but she had hoped that her husband might take on some of the household chores.

When it came time to decorate the baby's room she realized that her husband wasn't going to step up and do that either; so if she wanted it done, she would have to do it herself. She had to do everything from painting the walls to picking out the decorations and furniture. As much as she wanted her husband to take on more responsibility, she couldn't figure out a way to get him to do it. She had allowed him to set the boundaries that were comfortable for him and she hadn't pushed back earlier in the marriage so it was harder now for her to take that stand.

A year went by and she found out she was expecting her second child. When the second baby was born, she had the responsibility of going to work full time, taking care of two kids full time, and taking care of all the household responsibilities. She became more and more infuriated with her husband. Every time a new responsibility was added to the household, it became hers.

One day she decided to set up a college account for her kids. She was sitting in their home office filling out the paperwork and came across some unfamiliar documents. As she reviewed them in more detail, she realized they were credit card statements for numerous credit cards that her husband had opened up in his name. He had charged thousands in credit card debt, and because they were married, she was as liable financially as he was. For the sake of the kids she didn't want to get a divorce, but the possibility of a happy marriage now seemed impossible.

Kelly's Story

Kelly met a guy online. He was going through a divorce and had kids, but was separated from his wife. Like Nicole, she knew that he wasn't the perfect guy, but she told herself nobody was perfect and that in a relationship some give and take would always be required.

They started dating and my friend was so happy to be in a relationship. She had longed to be married and have a family of her own. He lived in the suburbs to be near his kids and she lived in the city. She spent a lot of time at his place, and once things started to get serious she bought a house in the suburbs to be closer to him. When his lease ended, he moved in with her.

She loves kids and was open to spending a lot of time with his, but made it very clear to him that she wanted kids of her own. Even though they weren't engaged, she trusted that he would propose and they would get married and start their own family. Meanwhile, she lost a lot of girlfriends because of her move to the suburbs; the distance made it more difficult to get together and she spent a significant amount of her time with her new boyfriend.

After a couple of years of dating, her boyfriend began to change. He didn't compliment her or tell her she looked beautiful, and she started to feel insecure about her appearance. He made comments about her looks and said she might consider losing a few pounds. This made her even more self-conscious. He made subtle hints about her weight, her outfit choices, and her grooming efforts ... and how all of those could be improved.

He no longer focused on all of the things that made her a unique, beautiful woman. He focused on the few physical attributes that in his mind made her less than the perfect girlfriend. After she had patiently dated him for more than three years, he still hadn't proposed. She found herself in a difficult position. Should she continue this relationship that she had already invested so much time in, hoping that her boyfriend would one day propose, or should she walk away and start over with someone else?

Esther's Story

My friend Esther was starting her senior year in college and had never dated. She had been heavily involved in sports, and dating wasn't her first priority. She was also focused on ensuring that her dating experiences were quality and didn't care much about the quantity. During her summer break she spent some time back home and met her first boyfriend.

She was intrigued that this guy was interested and she was looking forward to the opportunity of dating and experiencing her first relationship. Esther knew that this guy wasn't necessarily the type she wanted to invest a lot of time in when it came to potential for her future, but she liked the idea of being able to use the word "boyfriend." They enjoyed a short period of time together, but it wasn't long before she had to head back to college.

They never really had an opportunity to get to know each other because of the distance between them. They had some similar things in common and would try to share what was going on in their lives, but there was no depth in this relationship. They didn't really have anything solid upon which to establish a foundation. Unfortunately, the communication between them turned out to be terrible. They both had insecurities, and instead of being willing to show vulnerability and talking about how things made them feel, they brushed everything under the rug.

They gave it their best shot, but they were very young, and having a long-distance relationship turned out to be challenging for both of them. She was looking for someone who could meet her expectations physically, mentally, emotionally, and spiritually, and it was becoming clear he wasn't the one. After about three months, she broke up with him.

Miranda's Story

Another story is about my friend Miranda, who met a guy at a bar. They seemed to hit it off. She thought he was very attractive, they had great chemistry, and he made her laugh. When they started dating she realized that he drank a lot, but she ignored it.

At times he would drink a little too much and get loud and obnoxious, but he was still young and she figured he would settle down as he got a little older. The more time she spent with him the more her feelings grew, and she decided that this was someone she wanted to share her life with. After a year of dating, he proposed.

A year into their marriage, she realized that her husband was an alcoholic and needed help. He drank every day and when he got stressed out about work or other challenging things happening in his life, he drank excessively. He always wanted to go to the bar and she wanted to do other things. She didn't mind going to the bar occasionally, but she didn't want it to be the only place they went. She tried to encourage him to do things that would lessen his desire to drink.

She offered to go with him to get help, but he was convinced he didn't have a problem. She found herself fighting with him more often, and the fights usually started over something fairly stupid—like who was going to take the garbage out, how the eggs were pre-pared for breakfast, or not cleaning out the coffee pot.

She now knew that there were major problems in their relationship, but she felt that it was her responsibil-ity to stay with him and make it work. One night she was trying to find her keys and came across a small plastic bag in his jacket. In it was a white powdery substance, and although she had never done drugs, she recognized it was cocaine.

She flipped out. She immediately called him at work and asked him what it was doing in his jacket. He said he would talk to her when he got home. She was baffled. She knew that the drinking had been an issue, but drugs? That was unacceptable. When he got home he tried to brush the situation off as if it was no big deal. He said everybody has done drugs at some point in their lives and it wasn't like he did it all the time. He had gone out with some friends and they had it, so he decided to do it with them. He convinced her that it was actually just that one time.

As time went on, she realized that it wasn't just that one time and she confronted him again. This time their fight escalated quickly and he got so angry with her that he shoved her against the wall, pressing his fingertips into her collarbone and screaming in her face that he was a man and could do whatever he wanted to do. When he finally walked away and let her go, the weight of her body slithered along the wall until she reached the floor. She was stunned. She sat there sobbing uncontrollably, trying to comprehend what had just happened to her. How could this man she loved, and who she thought loved her, do something like this?

All of these women saw signs of trouble, of having chosen the wrong guy, and ignored them. In order to be able to lose the wrong guy, when you see signs like these you have to be strong enough to walk away. Whether you are dating, engaged, or married, when the relationship is detrimental to your emotional, mental, or physical well-being, it's time to end it.

When I was in my early twenties, I didn't have it in me to walk away from a bad relationship, but now I could easily do it. As you mature and gain dating experience, your tolerance for certain behaviors decreases. The most important lesson to learn is to value yourself and make sure that anyone who is in a relationship with you values you just as much.

Once you make the decision to walk away, you have to be strong enough to *never* go back. If you go back, as much as you think you have experienced the worst with that wrong guy, he will surprise you with even more. Those types of behaviors escalate over time. You do not want to experience this yourself in order to learn the lesson.

Once you leave, these types of men usually realize what they had and will do everything in their power to get you back. They will make empty promises, they will pretend to seek help, and they will lie over and over again until they get you back. Then things will go back to the way they were, or get even worse. Don't fall for it.

When you find Mr. Right, he will likely have some issues and things he needs to improve, but when you bring them to his attention he will not resist bettering himself; he will want to become the best man he can be for you. It's true that nobody is perfect and no relationship will be perfect, but you don't have to compromise who you are for anyone.

When you make the choice to allow any man into your life, you should know the boundaries you have in place for that relationship. You should never excuse unwanted behavior, especially if it's abusive. You deserve to be treated with respect, esteem, and dignity.

Assignment

Ask yourself these questions:

- Does my gut tell me that there is something wrong?
- Are the people around me (family and friends) warning me that this may not be the right guy?
- Do I feel like I'm walking on eggshells to avoid certain topics or conversations that might trigger unwanted behavior?
- Is it less stressful to be alone or with this person?
- Have I lost all desire to grow or improve myself?
- Do I behave differently in front of my friends when I'm around him?
- Do I have a hard time completely trusting him?
- Does it seem like I've given up a lot to be with him?
- Do I often feel like he's criticizing me and have to defend my behavior?
- Do I feel responsible for my partner's happiness?

- Do I prioritize this new relationship over older (maybe more important) relationships?
- Do I feel like I'm not being heard?
- When it comes to having those difficult real-life conversations, do I feel he checks out?

Whether it's verbal, emotional, physical, sexual, or any other type of abuse, you should never tolerate it. There is no excuse for letting another person's behavior put you in a situation that makes you feel less valuable than you are.

Our lives are what we make of them. We only get one life and usually it goes by much faster than we anticipate, so rather than put off until tomorrow what you could do today, live today and every one that follows like it's your last. Remove your rose-colored glasses to see the reality of your relationships, and if you don't like the picture you see, change it.

You must live in the present,
launch yourself on every
wave, find your eternity in
each moment. Fools stand on
their island of opportunities
and look toward another land.
There is no other land; there is
no other life but this.
—Henry David Thoreau

8

Decide How Tall He Needs to Be ... to "Ride This Ride"

We live in a society that provides immediate gratification. We can get food and alcohol delivered to our door. We can swipe right on a dating application and get a date or sex within a very short time. We can shop using credit to increase our buying power. We can hop in an Uber to a nightclub and reinvent our world within minutes. We can liposuction our way to a new body. Most people don't like waiting for anything, and some people prefer to find a new person to date rather than invest time and effort in bettering their existing relationship. It's not always easy to discipline yourself to make the best choices for your life.

Ensuring that your boyfriend, hangout guy, Friday night sex partner, or potential mate has all the right characteristics to suit you will require a commitment and some time, but it will also have a major impact on the quality of your life. There are those who might be looking for Mr. Right Now, and that's perfectly fine if you can emotionally handle the act of sex without any ties. Others of us are looking for Mr. Right, and it's important that we keep our standards at the appropriate level to ensure our relationships will be successful.

Take a moment to think about your past dating relationships. Then consider the types of guys you're dating now and your current relationships. Do you have a specific height requirement or specific look you prefer? Do you refuse to date a guy that smokes? How have you been treated by the guys you date? Do you feel lucky to be with them? Do you feel like they are lucky to be with you? Do you set standards to ensure that you are treated appropriately in your relationships? A lot of women feel they can mold and adjust their guy to be what they want him to be, but it's not true.

Bonnie's Story

Bonnie is currently single. Her worst relationship was with a guy who was nine years older. She liked that he was interested even though she was younger. She also liked that he was tall, dark, handsome, and well off. He had a nice car, a boat, and a nice house with a two-car garage. Bonnie thought he could take care of her and be a good provider. He had everything except the girl, and Bonnie believed she could fit perfectly into his life and they could be one happy family.

He was also appealing to her as a father figure since she hadn't had one while growing up. She liked that he could take care of her and she could lean on him. He was the older male figure who was lacking in her life ... more like a provider than a father, but something she was looking for and in need of at that time.

What she overlooked was his personality. He had a tendency to belittle her because he was older. He did have more experience, and he believed he was smarter than she was. He constantly told her that she was inexperienced because she was young.

One time they went to a comedy show and she laughed a lot. To her this was appropriate—it was a comedy show, after all—but he told her she was acting childish. If she did anything he didn't like or acted in a way he didn't agree with, he told her she was too young.

Bonnie was looking for the guy who could rescue her, and she wanted to be able to just move into his house and start a family. He knew kids were a passion of hers but didn't know if he wanted them himself. Bonnie thought he might never want to get married or have kids; he just liked having her as a showpiece. She was pretty and young and he probably thought others would be impressed that he could get someone like her. Unfortunately he didn't value Bonnie and make her feel like she was important to him. He was manipulative too.

Bonnie wasn't really living in his house, but she was staying there most nights. He didn't trust her enough to give her a key so she had to wait for him to come home in order to get into his place. One day she was at an office Christmas party and realized she had left her phone at his house. She called him from work and told him where she was and that she had left her phone behind, and let him know she wouldn't get back until about 10:00 p.m. He told her that was no problem, but when she got back to his place she could tell something was wrong with her phone. She soon realized he had been making calls and looking through her texts. When she confronted him, he lied, denying it.

Unfortunately for him, he couldn't control his frustration so he ended up confronting her about things he had seen in her call history and text messages. Bonnie had been going to country music concerts; he didn't want to go because he thought that was for younger people. He asked why she was texting about the shows. She wasn't doing anything wrong, but he had convinced himself that Bonnie was interested in someone else; a group of them had been going to concerts together and there were guys in that group. She tried to explain to him that she wasn't interested in any other guys. She tried to reassure him that all communications with any of the guys from the group were only about the concerts she was attending with the group.

But this guy had a friend who worked at the police department and he printed out Bonnie's phone records to show her how much she had been texting one guy from the group. She was surprised that he would go to such lengths. Then he told her she had twenty minutes to pack all of her stuff and leave. She couldn't believe the way he was reacting when nothing had ever happened. She packed and went back to her mom's.

About two weeks after she left, she was planning to go to another concert with the same group of people. He had looked up their schedule and showed up at Bonnie's mom's house the same night, knowing Bonnie wouldn't be home but asking to see her. He told her mom he wanted to get back together with Bonnie and he ended up manipulating that situation with her mom, trying to make her believe it hadn't been his fault that they broke up. Unfortunately, Bonnie didn't get along well with her mom; she took his side and blamed Bonnie for their breakup. He had already made up his mind and didn't want to hear Bonnie's side, and he took it a step further and smeared Bonnie's name with his cousin (who was Bonnie's coworker at the time) and his mom. Bonnie didn't appreciate the way he behaved in the end, but it shouldn't have surprised her—he had done the same during their relationship.

He was so jealous and controlling, and Bonnie eventually realized that she didn't want to deal with that negative behavior for the rest of her life. She tried so hard to please him, thinking that if she could do certain things to make him happy—clean his house, take care of him, and make him happy sexually—it would eventually make him love her enough to want to marry her and start a family. She thought that her love could change him. She thought her actions could convince him to change his mind. She compromised a lot. She let him call her names. She agreed to run errands and not have a key to his house. She allowed him to belittle her because she wanted to prove her love to him, but she learned through that relationship that any guy who belittles her does not value her and isn't worthy of her love. She also learned that if a guy isn't ready to be married and have kids, there is nothing she can do to convince him.

Fortunately, she was strong enough to walk away. Later, she saw him at a funeral with his new girlfriend. He hadn't known Bonnie was going to be there, and she could tell he was trying to talk to her. Later he reached out to Bonnie and said he wanted to get married and have kids, but she knew that was a lie—he'd had time to try to make contact with her and make things right but he never did. He's continued to reach out to Bonnie about once a year since their breakup, but she no longer pays any attention to him.

Sarah's Story

Sarah was in a relationship that initially provided immediate gratification. But after a period of time it turned into an abusive relationship. Her guy checked all the boxes: handsome, good job, great personality, and the chemistry they shared was undeniable. Sarah did her best to make the relationship work, but when she realized that the abuse would continue she knew she had to end it.

Sarah was smart; she learned a very valuable lesson through that relationship—how to qualify potential men before dating them. She kept her radar up and looked at every little thing very carefully, paying attention to details she had never cared to notice before. At first she overreacted if she saw any signs of anger at all, but over time she learned to be protective without being too sensitive.

Her pattern was to not sleep with men easily. Setting this boundary allowed her to be less emotionally involved and to see the men she dated more clearly. It was important for her to see their kindness and gentleness as real characteristics in their personality. She never set herself up to anger potential guys just to see a reaction, but she was always alert for it. Personal control was a major issue for her, and she needed to ensure that anyone she dated could be in control of his own emotions while disagreeing. Ultimately, she figured out that disagreements may lead to heated discussions, but nothing about that behavior is abusive. She came to realize it's natural for people to disagree and the important thing is that both sides can communicate and come to some sort of resolution. She navigated more and more to personalities that were more peaceful, kind, loving, and gentle versus outgoing, gregarious, or the life of the party.

At a deep level, Sarah was becoming more empowered. She had been a doormat in that abusive relationship—she couldn't be right because he had to be right.
This led to feelings of resentment and anger and corro-
sive issues on Sarah's part. She kept stuffing everything
inside instead of figuring out how to fight fair, which
she learned was important in relationships: if you don't
do that, one party won't get the resolution they need,
and that doesn't help to build the relationship.

After that bad relationship, Sarah dated another guy
who had a drug problem, but she soon recognized that
she needed to get away from that relationship entirely.
She was smart enough at that point to know that drug
problems often lead to abusive relationships.

Sarah feels that if you are in a relationship, you are
never who you are by yourself. Your attention always
has to be on "the other." Now that she's married, if
her husband isn't the most important thing in her life
grid, their marriage suffers. Having a healthy, whole
relationship involves respect for who each other is and
what each other wants. Sarah's husband and she don't
focus on material things but on lasting values. This
helps them see the things that are really important and
takes their focus off those things that are a part of life
but not their priority.

Sarah understands coupling is coupling and never
done in isolation. Most people change throughout their
lives, and when you are in a relationship both of you

have to make adjustments. Sarah's husband and she have both changed throughout the course of their marriage, and on multiple occasions have had to reexamine their relationship and decide what they want it to look like going forward. In Sarah's view, it's the only way to have a fulfilling marriage. Any marriage can last, but not all are fulfilling.

It's essential that we learn from our mistakes and invest time to ensure our dating is more focused on quality than on quantity. In our younger years, we may think that being asked out on a date is exciting and validates our self-worth. As we get older, we may decide that our time is too important to waste on a date that we know has zero possibility of growing into something more.

It's important to accept that, in general, people can change if they set their minds to it, but that most of our characteristics, ideologies, beliefs, and personality traits remain consistent throughout or lives. Understanding this will help you better qualify any potential guys you may consider dating.

If a guy really likes sports and wants to watch the pre-game, every moment of the live game, and then keeps the same channel on to catch all of the highlights of the post-game, no matter how much he likes you, he's still going to make watching sports his priority. If a guy loves to play golf and enjoys spending most of his weekends on the golf course, you aren't going to be able to change that about him.

When you start dating someone, you always put your best foot forward and make sacrifices so you can spend time with the other person and get to know each other. It's an exciting time, it's something new, feelings and emotions are intense, butterflies happen, and the possibility of love makes you forget what your day-to-day life looked like before you met each other. All of your priorities shift then and friends, family, and work typically take a back seat.

Once the newness of the relationship starts to fade and you plan to be together on a long-term basis, you will both likely realize that all of the sacrifices you have been making are going to require some adjustments. This is the phase of your relationship when you realize that some of the other person's priorities aren't the same as yours and both of you are going to have to make some compromises if you are still going to be able to spend time together.

Let's consider the avid sports fan scenario. This guy may decide that he doesn't need to watch the pre-game and post-game unless he's out with the boys for the night. He may agree to limit his sports watching to just the live games. He may even invite you to watch the games with him to make you feel more involved in his life. The guy who loves to golf may decide to catch an early tee-time on Saturday so he can finish his eighteen holes by early afternoon and still have time to spend with you on Saturday evening.

You will obviously have to make some adjustments as well. You may need to limit watching romantic comedies, *Real Housewives*, *Teen Mom*, and *The Bachelor* as your evening entertainment after work and incorporate some new shows from Spike, TNT, and ESPN.

The bottom line is that being in a relationship requires adjustments, and both of you will need to determine what those adjustments will be.

Avid Sports Fan—Wrong Guy

Typically the wrong guy is selfish and doesn't want to adjust any of his "guy" time to be with you. He will spend hours on end with his guys watching sports and then call you up about 10 p.m. to ask to come over so he can spend time with you. This way he doesn't have to make any sacrifices. It also conveniently puts him in a position to visit you when it's late and close to your bedtime, so he can get the added benefit of sex. He will even try to convince you that he is making sacrifices by coming over to see you because the guys were still hanging out and didn't want him to leave (as if he was doing you a favor by coming over to be with you).

Golf Lover—Wrong Guy

The wrong guy who loves to golf will play almost all day on Saturday and then give you a call when it's too dark to play. He'll make you feel like he sacrificed his time to be with you on Saturday evening because the guys were still at the club smoking cigars and playing poker. Then, just when you think you've got the rest of the weekend to spend with him, he jumps out of bed at 5 a.m. on Sunday to make his early tee-time at the course.

Avid Sports Fan—Mr. Right

When you find Mr. Right, there will still be sacrifices and compromise, but it won't feel difficult. For both of you, the goal will be to make each other happy. Mr. Right will limit his sports watching time and he'll invite you to watch some games with him. He will talk to you throughout the game and explain the plays. He'll share with you the reason he loves watching sports and it will help you realize why it's important to him.

If he's really smart, he'll figure out how the game relates to something you really like and try to show you the similarities so you can appreciate the game too. It will become something you enjoy doing together and not a complete sacrifice on your part every time a game comes on. Occasionally, if he has to miss a game or the two of you are running late and don't catch the opening play, he won't freak out and blame you for making him miss his beloved sports time.

Golf Lover—Mr. Right

Mr. Right who loves to golf will buy you a set of clubs and some cute golf attire and invite you to play with him at the club. He'll teach you how to swing, let you drive the cart, and treat for lunch to make it special rather than his own private quiet time on the course. Mr. Right will always do his best to figure out a way to let you be a part of his life and share it with him, rather than figuring out ways to have his own time away from you. Even though you both should still have time to do things alone, or with the girls and guys, it's important that Mr. Right wants to be with you more often than he wants to be without you.

I mentioned Patti Stanger's book *Become Your Own Matchmaker* in a previous chapter. She recommends making a list of what your exes have in common and what you liked and didn't like about them. Based on those answers, she suggests creating your top ten criteria for your Mr. Right. Some women have unrealistic goals when it comes to finding their Mr. Right. They have seventy-two items on their list of criteria and wonder why *no* man can meet their expectations. Patti advises that having a top ten is reasonable.

You are never going to find the perfect guy, but you will be able to find the perfect guy for you. It's important to consider who he is when you meet him. You need to realize that even if he's Mr. Right and is willing to make sacrifices to be with you, who he is won't change. He's going to continue to be the same man throughout his life and you need to determine if that's the person you want to spend the rest of your life with.

Relationship Considerations

Consider some of the things that may not surface until later in the relationship. Are you a cat person while he's a dog person? This can work, but are you willing to have two pets in the house that may not get along? Is he an early riser but you like to sleep until noon? If he's worked out and is on his third cup of coffee on a Saturday morning while you're still trying to figure out if you want to get out of bed, this may require a little bit more compromise for both of you when it comes to sharing time together.

Is he a fly-by-the-seat-of-his-pants type of guy, always wanting to be spontaneous, while you're an organized planner and it's uncomfortable for you to not know what's happening next or when you will be sitting down to have dinner? This is definitely something you can work through together, but it may require you to become a little more spontaneous and him a little less. Is he Jewish and you are Catholic? This may not seem like a big deal at all if neither one of you are very religious or attend services on a weekly basis, but if you get married and have kids you will need to figure which religion you will teach them.

Earlier I mentioned that I was engaged to a guy who was Jewish and I am a Christian, and we decided to call off our engagement because we couldn't figure out a way to compromise either of our religious beliefs enough to make it work for our future children. This was a very helpful learning experience for me; I had the opportunity through dating to realize that my Mr. Right needs to be a Christian.

I didn't fully understand how important my faith was to me until I was challenged to let go of it to some degree. I think dating can be a wonderful experience for women who are trying to figure out who they are and what they want out of life. When you get out and meet new people, it exposes you to new things, new ways of living, new cultures, and new experiences. If you go into dating with an open mind and allow the journey to be just as important as the outcome of finding Mr. Right, I think you will gain new perspective and a broader outlook about life.

I've been able to establish a new set of criteria for finding my Mr. Right based on things I have learned from dating in the past. I once met a guy who wasn't a Christian, and given my engagement experience, I knew that his being Christian was a critical consideration for me. I dismissed him, but he was persistent, and I finally shared my experience with him and the reason I wasn't interested in dating him. He wasn't willing to give up that easily.

Guys can be very determined to get what they want. He agreed to go to church with me one Sunday. He showed an interest in Christianity and continued to attend services with me for several months. The church we were attending offered a six-week class that taught Christianity and what it means to be a Christian. We attended the class together and a short time after that he became a Christian.

Your guy may not make the decision to become what you need just so he can be with you, but the important thing to remember is to not compromise who you are for anyone. It's necessary for everyone to compromise if they are going to be in a relationship, but recognize the difference between compromising *things you do* and *who you are.*

Assignment

Take some time to think about what type of person you will consider dating. It's important to be honest with yourself when you start setting these expectations.

- Is it reasonable to want a guy who has rock-hard abs when your muffin top is a bit larger than you would like it to be?
- Would it be fair to expect to date a guy who looks like a supermodel when you are a seven?
- Would it be open-minded of you to expect your guy to make six figures when you only make five?

Being reasonable with expectations will help you be successful in determining which guys have potential for you and which guys don't.

No one can

MAKE

you feel

INFERIOR

without your

CONSENT

9

Set Boundaries ... Love Is Not Always a Feeling— It Can Be a Decision

Have you heard the expression "Love is not a feeling—it's a decision"? Some people think that love is a feeling and if they fall out of love with a person, they no longer have to be with them.

Consider a relationship between a parent and a child. A newborn gives nothing to the parent; the relationship is very one-sided. The baby needs to be fed and clothed, have its diapers changed, and be soothed when upset. It requires full-time care, attention, affection, and love.

During this time, the parent chooses to love the child, understanding that at some point in the near future, the baby will recognize who they are and be able to give back to them as part of the relationship: the first smile, the first laugh, the first finger grip, the first hug, the first cuddle. When the child reaches a certain age and begins testing boundaries, parents make a choice to discipline their children as an act of love.

Setting boundaries and disciplining children may not be easy for parents, but they realize that in order for the child to be healthy and socialized with others, and because they love them, they have to discipline them. As the years go by and the parents get older, this relationship may shift again and the child may have to be the one who chooses to love and take care of their parents because they can no longer take care of themselves.

Disciplined Love

Keep this perspective in mind as you think about your experiences dating guys or being in relationships. How many times have you allowed the feeling of falling in love to overwhelm you to the point where you let go of all caution, reason, and logic? How many times has that choice led to heartache in the end? Don't get me wrong—falling in love is one of the most desired and beautiful gifts we have the opportunity to experience. But when you let your emotions dictate your actions, you are likely setting yourself up for disaster.

If you make the choice to love someone (even when they aren't acting the way you want them to act), it makes that person trust that you are going to be there for them even when times get tough. If you know that this person is going to choose to love you as well, and not possibly fall out of love with you and leave at any given time, it creates a stable environment to allow the relationship to grow and blossom.

Accountability

Most of us aren't excited about the idea of account-ability. We want the freedom to do whatever we want, whenever we want, regardless of what it costs anyone around us.

Fortunately, our lives are usually structured in a way that will not allow us to get out of control with our selfish desires. Our parents raise us with a set of values that limit us from having full freedom. Our siblings ensure that whatever we get (reward or discipline) is fairly equal within the family confines. Our friends have their own set of standards that we need to abide by in order to maintain friendships. Our potential mates require us to put our best foot forward to make the idea of starting a relationship with them worthwhile.

We all have accountability to someone to one degree or another, and for the most part it protects us from becoming destructive to ourselves or others. But some of us lose that accountability along the way, for many dif-ferent reasons, and we become dangerous to ourselves or we allow others to be a danger to us.

Being accountable to others provides a second degree of protection for us, but the primary objective should be accountability to ourselves. We should value ourselves enough to make choices that directly affect our lives in a way that builds up who we are and doesn't tear us down. We should value ourselves enough to never let anyone else affect the quality of our lives.

Hopefully by now you have established a solid criteria base for your relationships and understand that choosing to love a potential Mr. Right is much more time effective than choosing to love the wrong guy who had a bad past and continues to use that as an excuse for the way he is now.

I haven't always made the best decisions about who I choose to love, but I am proud to say that each experience has molded me into the strong, no-nonsense, stand-up-for-myself, and demand-the-love-and-respect-I-deserve-out-of-relationships woman that I am today.

Cindy and Jacob

My girlfriend Cindy dated Jacob, who had previously been married. He told her that he had made some mistakes in his first marriage but had learned from them and was at a place in his life where he wanted to be in a serious relationship. She didn't feel right judging him about his past, especially when he was trying to make a fresh start.

At the same time, she moved forward with caution because she wanted to make sure that Jacob's intent was truly to do his best to be her Mr. Right, and that he had really learned from his first failed marriage. So many men talk the talk, but if their actions don't line up, you shouldn't trust what they say.

One of the things that Cindy really liked about Jacob was the relationship he had with his daughter. For a long time, she had chosen not to date men with children because of the baggage that comes with those relationships: dealing with exes, limited choices on where you can live, child support, co-parenting, and all the rest. But now she had reached a point in her life where most men her age had children, so she was open to it.

The first time she saw them together, she could see the love Jacob had for his daughter. It really impressed her that he was able to show so much love while at the same time not being afraid to discipline her. She loved that his daughter loved and respected him, and she was well-behaved.

Although Cindy didn't have any children of her own, she had a pretty good idea of how she planned to raise them. A part of her was glad that Jacob had a child and she could see what type of dad he was with his daughter, and could potentially be with her children.

Children and Dating

So many people who are dating don't invest the time to talk about important things like how they plan to raise their children. This shouldn't be a topic of discussion when you first start dating someone, but when things start to get serious, these are absolutely necessary discussions to have before taking a step toward marriage.

If you don't think children should be spanked and the person you are dating is a firm believer in spanking, it's a good idea to talk that through before you get married. If you aren't able to come to a compromise before you have children, it will become a constant battle between the two of you in front of the children. Parents who are not on the same page about disciplining their children have a very hard time convincing their children that they are aligned and have agreement as the authority figures. The children will play one parent against the other, which can create a very stressful household.

As time went on, Cindy started to realize that Jacob talked more about the things he would do with his daughter than actually doing them. This was subtle because Jacob had his daughter every other weekend, so when he talked about taking her shopping or baking cookies with her, it wasn't clear right away that these activities were actually few and far between. Their weekends would get busy with normal day-to-day activities, and there wasn't always time for father and daughter bonding time.

Jacob talked about his daughter's mother and said she wasn't a good mom and wasn't taking care of their daughter the way she should. Cindy later realized that this was Jacob's attempt to make himself look better, and that his ex was actually a very good mom. There were times when Jacob wanted to have a couple of drinks after work with the guys and she offered to watch their daughter until Jacob was ready to pick her up. This wouldn't have been a big deal to Cindy on any given night, but Jacob did this during the few nights he had her every other weekend and she thought he should make his daughter a higher priority. It had become clear to Cindy that Jacob wasn't the great father that she had originally thought. She came to realize that he didn't respect his daughter's mother, he didn't respect his own mother, and he was starting to lose respect for her.

Cindy's decision to break things off with Jacob was not easy because she had become very close with his daughter and loved her like her own. But she just couldn't look past the fact that Jacob would treat her children the same way if they ended up having children together. She decided that she wanted to be in a relationship with someone who treated her with the respect she deserved. Cindy wasn't looking forward to being alone again, but she knew she deserved better than what Jacob was willing to offer.

Trish and Bill

Trish met Bill when she was in her mid-thirties after she had been divorced from her first husband for six years. They spent about a year and a half together becoming really good friends before they felt that first spark of chemistry. They worked together, so they had an easy platform to get to know each other without rushing into things. After Trish's divorce, she wanted to build the foundation of all future relationships and get to know any potential guys very well before she fell in love. She believed this was an ideal scenario for relationships to be successful. After he realized that Trish was the one, Bill proposed, and they were able to enjoy a successful relationship and remained committed in their marriage. They had difficult times, but nothing they couldn't get through.

After they had been married for several years, an infidelity occurred that never became physical; Bill had become emotionally attached to another woman. Trish and Bill separated for several months and were able to work through it. Trish wasn't sure that she could have successfully gone through that devastating experience with anyone else, but Bill was completely honest with her from the very beginning. Honesty is very important to Trish, and she really appreciated Bill's willingness to share his unfaithful actions with her..

As much as Trish was caught off guard, Bill shared with her that he had not been prepared for what transpired and he was trying to figure out how it happened as well. As a couple, they both worked toward figuring out how this event had come about in their marriage. Although it may have seemed obvious to an outsider that Bill was the person at fault because he had the connection with another woman, infidelity in any manner is very rarely the fault of one person. Trish and Bill realized they had stopped communicating, and they explored any other things in their relationship that had

caused Bill to look elsewhere. They did some couples'
counseling because both of them wanted their marriage
to work. They hadn't married until about four years
into their relationship, but they wanted their marriage
to succeed.

Through the process of counseling and learning
about the gaps that they had both allowed into their
marriage, Trish found absolute conviction in the power
of forgiveness. There is a palpable power when you
forgive someone, and she did forgive him, entirely and
completely... and Bill forgave her for things too. Trish
is happy that she and Bill have been rock solid ever
since in terms of working stuff out instead of avoiding
the challenges in their relationship.

Their counselor was an important piece of their
effective communication because for a while, they
couldn't talk to each other. Communication wholeness
comes from a community of perspectives—friends,
family, counselors and other outside sources. Not all
advice shared is going to be good, but the good and
bad outside communication resources helped them
both balance their own viewpoints and make their own
decisions. The process involved weighing all aspects
of the relationship, internalizing their own feelings,
praying for wisdom, and ultimately trusting their own
intuition as to whether they wanted to go through it and
what they wanted their end result to be. They had to
make a hard choice to commit to making the relationship better, and they had to have accurate, measurable

results as outcomes of their choices. Trish knew she didn't want counseling forever; she wanted resolution. She and Bill are happily married today because of the decision they made to love each other even though it took dedication and determination to get through a very difficult situation.

Lauren and Don

Lauren met Don when she was in her early thirties. She had been through several relationships before Don, but none of the guys were Christian and she had bad experiences with them mistreating her or letting her down. Lauren met Don at a church event, and she was excited to have the opportunity to date a Christian—she knew dating in a Christian context would be very different. Don proved her right. When he asked Lauren to be his girlfriend, he said that she would first and foremost be his sister in Christ. Don told Lauren that he wanted to respect her, and his words and actions set a precedent for their relationship. It made Lauren feel very valued.

Lauren was physically attracted to Don, but it wasn't primarily about the physicality as it had been for her in past relationships. She had never felt respected and valued as a person the way she did with Don. He never pressured her to make out with him or sleep with him. In Lauren's past relationships she had sometimes used her sexual appeal to lengthen the relationship. Now, it was nice to not have the pressure of being good enough or having someone want her enough to stay in the relationship.

She and Don were intentional about spending time together. They tried to do things that kept them from staying home and having that temptation that may lead into other things. They went to dinner together, they volunteered together, and sometimes served together at church. They often went to a party at a friend's house, where they could meet and interact with other people. Having that time to be together with friends, or being alone but investing a lot of time in getting to know each other and talking, made Lauren feel like she was in a real relationship. By sharing a lot of time doing things together, they had the opportunity to get to know each other better. They also enjoyed doing new things together and it allowed them to be in new environments where they got to learn new things about each other. Lauren and Don dated for about eight months, but ultimately discovered they weren't the best fit for each other and decided to break up. Lauren is still looking for her Mr. Right, but she's grateful for the experience of having someone love her intentionally.

Don't Settle for Less

Have you ever settled for less than what you deserve just so you have someone around? This could apply to family, friends, or dating relationships. Sometimes we prefer having an unhealthy relationship to being alone.

One thing every person has in common is that they want to be loved and accepted; nobody wants to feel alone or left out. It takes a strong person to make the choice to be alone rather than accept less than they deserve. Don't let the fear of being alone ever stop you from standing up for who you are and all that you deserve.

Think about your relationships, past and present. What areas have you been really strong in and what areas have you struggled with repeatedly? What can you do to strengthen those areas of weakness and become a better version of you?

You have to be willing to do the best thing for you, regardless of how it may affect the other person involved. At times this may mean being strong enough to make the choice to be alone, the choice not to settle.

Assignment

Ask youself these questions:

- What do you do well in relationships?
- What qualities and unique characteristics do you have to offer?
- How strong is your ability to be true to yourself?
- What do other people see as your strengths?
- What values and ethics set you apart?
- What are your negative relationship habits?
- Are there patterns in past relationships that you can't seem to navigate away from?
- Are you willing to invest the appropriate amount of time to make a relationship work?
- Do you share your feelings freely and require others to be sensitive to your needs?
- What negative feedback have you received from past relationships?

When it comes to dating and relationships, love can be a decision—it doesn't always have to be based on a feeling. What decision will you make today to influence the way you are loved in the future?

Every woman that finally
figured out her worth, has
picked up her suitcases of
pride and boarded a flight to
freedom, which landed in the
valley of change.
—Shannon Adler

Never give up

10

Do Whatever It Takes ... to Get What You Deserve

When you think about relationships in your life that haven't been successful, do you place the blame on the person you were dating, on yourself, or on both parties? Relationships rarely fall apart because of one person. Although it's tempting to want to place the blame on someone else, it's much more beneficial to look back at the relationship and be open to the truth.

I've had relationships end because of someone else's faults, because of my own faults, and because of the faults of both of us. One thing I've always tried to do is learn from each experience. It's valuable to take the time to figure out why you broke up, what you didn't like about the relationship, and whether your criteria have changed for any future relationships. If you don't

149

learn those key things from each relationship, you will likely fall into a pattern of dating the wrong guy.

Another idea to keep in mind is that you don't want to jump into a new relationship until you are completely over the one you just walked away from, or that walked away from you. If you start a new relationship while you're still feeling broken, you will likely have challenges, and 99 percent of the time the new guy isn't going to have what it takes to fix your brokenness. Take some time to heal, accept the blame if you were part of the reason the relationship ended and accept the loss if you weren't ready for the relationship to end. Only then, when you are happy and content with being alone, is it time to search for Mr. Right.

So many relationships fail because people are not feeling whole and content when they get into them. They expect the other person to fill the void. Even if you were the one who ended the last one and feel great and ready to date again, it's a good idea to spend a little time alone and appreciate the freedom of being single. If you find yourself always leaving the relationship in advance of being the one who gets hurt, you may want to consider that repetitive behavior and determine whether you are bringing all of you into your relationships.

Janice and Jack

When Janice and Jack got married they were both broken, each in their own way. She had been sexually abused as a child and he was insecure. Janice had turned off a lot of her emotions, and her sexual, emotional, and mental boundaries had been skewed by the abuse. Jack longed to be loved, and when he was growing up his family had a tendency to do whatever it took to keep the peace, even if that meant lying to each other.

For a long time Janice blamed Jack for not being what she needed and lacked as a person; he was always wrong for falling short. But she went through some counseling and realized that she herself had a lot of problems, related to the abuse. Janice could no longer blame him for everything. She had to take some accountability for the emotional impacts of what had happened to her, even though it was not her choice and by no means her fault. Janice and Jack struggled to fix themselves for a long time. They finally made a breakthrough when they went to couples' counseling, and both realized that they needed to make adjustments within themselves to make their marriage work. Neither one of them was perfect, and they had to understand each other's needs in order to be genuinely happy and make the marriage successful.

Janice shared with me an interesting thing she thinks about marriage—that it's like being naked in front of a mirror all the time. When you're single, it's easy to feel like you've got everything together and nothing you do is wrong because you are the only one judging your reflection. By contrast, being married gives both spouses repeated opportunities to judge their reflections—the good and the bad. It makes it very difficult to hide your flaws from your spouse. When your spouse is not content in the marriage, they are more likely to see the bad and point it out. And it's not easy to hear that type of criticism from someone you love, someone who is supposed to love you unconditionally as well.

Jack and Janice both realized that insecurity was a destructive thread that had woven its way through their marriage. They both acted out and became defensive because neither one of them wanted to be hurt by the other. The worst attributes in both of them turned out to be what each of them desperately needed to help their own insecurities. She lacked emotion because of the abuse, and all he wanted was to feel loved. Jack lied at times to keep the peace, and all Janice wanted was honesty and security. Through many years of counseling, they both overcame their insecurities.

Their marriage wasn't perfect or easy, but the love that they had for each other and for their family motivated them to persevere. It was a rewarding experience for them to keep their commitment to each other. There is something that happens throughout the course of a relationship when all of the bad (and good) has happened and the two people are left standing together side by side. A level of strength and foundation exists in that relationship that doesn't exist in most other marriages where people are willing to give up so easily. In not settling for less than both of them deserved, Jack and Janice learned what a successful marriage looked like, and they are proud that their children today have the foundation they do because of it, and have solid, strong families of their own.

Today, Janice is a couples counselor. Looking back, she admits that had she been the premarital counselor to herself and Jack, she would not have recommended marriage. She tells the couples she counsels that the best marriages are made when two people who are whole join together, not when two people are broken and need to fix themselves during the marriage.

Janice's abuse as a child greatly impacted her ability to be the wife Jack hoped she would be, as well as any chance of her having a successful marriage with any husband, no matter how wonderful he might have been. Even though abuse is evil and Janice would never wish for anyone to have to go through it, she now uses her story to help others. She wants people to know that out of those ashes can emerge hope and beauty. A lot of people have experienced abuse, and it's nothing to be ashamed of or hide. Admitting that it happened; forgiving the abuser; forgiving yourself for thinking it may have been your fault, or for any ways you have wronged others as a result of the abuse; and allowing positivity to fill that negative void all provide people with the opportunity to experience a whole new way of living. Doing this work lets you become whole, love others, and allow others to love you. It's an incredibly rewarding process for those who are strong enough to dig through the trenches of the past.

Ana and Javier

Javier and Ana got married in their early twenties and had two beautiful daughters. They had been married for almost twenty years when Ana decided it was time to get a divorce. Ana wasn't extremely unhappy in her marriage, but she had grown tired of being the one who had to take control and be responsible for everything. It wasn't that Javier wouldn't help out, but Ana had to direct everything and tell him what to do. He was the type of person who would often say, "Just tell me what to do and I'll do it." He wouldn't take charge, take the time to come up with strategies, or drive things. In Ana's opinion, marriage should be a partnership and hers wasn't. Instead she felt as if Javier was the third child they never wanted to have.

After struggling with the decision for many years, Ana finally came to the realization that she didn't respect Javier as a husband and partner. Everything was always on her shoulders, and if she was going to shoulder it all anyway, she would be happier doing it by herself. *If I can't enhance someone and they can't enhance me,* she thought, why be in a relationship?

It was not an easy decision for Ana because they had children and she seriously considered the negative impact it could have on them. At the same time, she didn't want to give her daughters the impression that her marriage was what a healthy one should look like, and she didn't want that type of relationship for them. She knew that if she continued in an unfulfilled marriage, she would end up not loving Javier at all and their relationship would be irreparable, which would ultimately be the worst outcome for them and their children. For Ana, it was very lonely being "married" yet feeling as though her husband was nowhere to be found, even though he was right there by her side.

Walking Away

It can be very difficult to walk away from a relationship, even a bad one. I've heard so many familiar stories from women who are in awful, unhealthy relationships, and when I ask, "Why don't you leave?" their response is always similar: "He had a bad past ... he really does love me ... I just love him so much I can't let him go ... he's not a bad person, he just has a bad temper ..." —and on and on. They make excuses because they believe that being alone will be worse than the negative things they are dealing with.

I've had enough experience to know that it is possible to be single and content, and it is a thousand times better than being in a relationship that doesn't give me everything I deserve. As much as I would love to be able to say that I learned this lesson easily and early on, it's not the case. I had to learn this through several bad relationships and over a longer period of time than I would have liked. The important thing is that I learned it, and it's a lesson that has made a huge difference in the way I live my life, the way I date and the types of relationships I allow in my life.

Trina and Jerry

One of my good friends, Trina, is now happily married but did her fair share of dating while she was single. She had been looking for a stable guy who would be good to her and commit, but she had a hard time getting past the initial attraction and chemistry she felt when first meeting a new guy. All too often, she found herself falling for the wrong one.

One thing I admire about Trina is that she appropriately demanded respect from men, guys and bosses alike. She understood that people could only treat her the way she allowed them to. She met Jerry, liked him immediately, and was drawn to the chemistry between them. Although she was extremely attracted to him, she did her due diligence and took the time to ensure that his actions spoke just as loud as his words.

After about six months, she was delighted to be dating Jerry because he was living up to every promise he had made. He was genuinely concerned about her feelings and went out of his way to make her feel special. He seemed head over heels in love with her. The good continued to outweigh the bad, and she was confident her future with Jerry was promising and would lead to a serious and long-term relationship, possibly even marriage.

A year and a half after they started dating, Jerry popped the question and they were engaged. Trina was so excited! She had the perfect guy. She had found her Mr. Right. But within a few months of the wedding, things started to change. Jerry started coming home from work late all the time, and he always had an excuse. Sometimes he blamed his tardiness on a long day at the office, sometimes on really bad traffic, sometimes a blown tire or running out of gas, and sometimes on just needing a little time alone.

Jerry also got calls from time to time and had to leave right away to meet one of his friends. Trina didn't quite understand why he needed to leave so abruptly, but he always had an excuse: my friend's car broke down, my friend and his wife just got into a big fight and he needs someone to talk to, or my friend's electric drill went out and he's in the middle of a big home improvement project.

She wanted to believe him, but it had gotten to a point where he was coming home later and later, and coming up with more and more excuses for why he needed to leave the house out of the blue. She knew in her gut he wasn't cheating on her, but she also knew something wasn't right. Trina decided the best course of action was to address it head on and just ask him directly. When Jerry got home that night she said she needed to talk to him, and asked him point blank why he was always working late and sometimes had to suddenly leave the house.

At first, he kept making excuses to justify his behavior, but she continued to press him until he reached his breaking point. Jerry sighed heavily with his head in his hands, stared down at the floor with utter embarrassment, and said, "I've got connections and ties that I can't break. I owe people and I don't have a way out." Trina was confused, trying to put together the pieces.

Nothing made sense about what he was saying so she asked him again.

"Jerry what is going on with you?"

"I'm trying to tell you," he said. "I'm trying to be honest with you. I hate all of the lies—they're eating away at me. I just didn't know how to tell you."

She kept pressing. "What, Jerry, what?"

"My family is in the mob," he said.

Her jaw dropped. She couldn't put any words together. She stared blankly at him, certain that this couldn't be the truth.

A thousand thoughts ran through her mind at once. She told herself that somewhere along the way, she would surely have seen the signs or figured it out—this must be a mistake. The tears rolled down Jerry's face as he shared all of the details about his family, the ties he had to the mob, the loyalty he owed to certain people who would never forgive him for turning his back on them, and the favors he owed to so many people who had helped him when he was in a tight spot.

Trina sat in disbelief. She couldn't believe what Jerry was saying, but at the same time in her gut, she knew it was true. The whole picture started to become clear. Every excuse, every late night, every little thing that she had told herself not to worry about—they were all attributed to this one big secret. How could they ever get past this? What would their future together look like? Could they still have a future together? Did she even want to continue being with a man who had lied to her all this time?

It seemed like they sat in silence for an eternity before she uttered the words, "I want a divorce." Jerry pleaded and begged for her to stay with him. He promised that he would figure out a way to get out and be a better man for her. She just couldn't accept it. She couldn't get past the big lie he had been telling her since the day they met.

A couple of days later, Trina was working from home when the doorbell rang. She went to answer it and found a large box sitting at the front door. She picked it up, noticing how light it felt, and carefully opened the top. She looked inside and found a tiny dead bird, its beady eyes staring up at her. She dropped the box and screamed, then immediately called Jerry at work and told him what she had found.

He told her everything would be fine and said he would leave work and head home right away. But by the time Jerry got home, it had become very clear who had delivered the dead bird: a member of Jerry's family had done it to send a clear message that Trina was part of the family now and had no choice but to stay with Jerry. As scared as Trina was, she wasn't about to let someone else determine her own fate. She knew Jerry wouldn't hurt her, but she was concerned that his family might just to keep her in check and ensure that nobody else would find out what Jerry had recently disclosed to her. She knew she had to make a plan to get out.

Abuse Should Not Be Excused

Experiences like Trina's may not be common, but there are plenty of women who have restraining orders against exes, are in protective custody because of abusive exes, and constantly live in fear of what may happen to them based on threats from their exes, whether husbands or boyfriends. Nobody should ever have to deal with any type of abuse or threat to their lives.

Stop believing the lies. Stop accepting the excuses. Accept the fact that if he hasn't changed by now, he's *not* going to. You can afford to leave him. Cut the cord. Dump the rogue! Those women who have left and persevered realize that it is possible to lose the wrong guy. They are able to enjoy a whole new way of living—freedom, happiness, joy, confidence, strong self-esteem, and contentment. It may not have been an easy journey, but these women are stronger, prouder, and more resilient because of those negative experiences.

Assignment

Look back at your last three relationships.
Think about how things ended ... and
why. Self-reflect and consider ways you
could have, would have, or should have
done things differently.
Ask yourself these questions:

- Did you tolerate unwanted behavior to
  keep the peace?
- Did you stay in the relationship longer
  than you should have, hoping that
  your ex would change?
- Did you make excuses for the way your
  ex treated you?
- Did you cause the breakup?
- What can you do differently in your
  next relationship to avoid these things
  happening again?

If you held on to the relationship a little
bit too long or were part of the reason the
relationship ended, don't beat yourself up.
Learn from these experiences so you don't
make the same mistakes again. Never give
up striving to be everything you know you

can be. Choose today to never stop trying
to find everything you've always wanted in
your Mr. Right.

If at first you don't succeed,
try, try again.
—William Edward Hickson

11

Plan Your Dream Vacation
... for One

D o you ever wish you had extra time in your day? Would you pay hard-earned money for a few extra hours spent doing something you love? Being single offers you the gift of time. It opens up a whole new world of discovering you: what you like, what you enjoy doing in your free time, where you want to travel, what music pleases you, and most importantly, the things you love about yourself. When we invest all our time in relationships, we don't invest in or learn about ourselves.

Self-Reflection
After a very emotional breakup, I made the decision to focus on myself. I took a little time to reflect on what went wrong, why it went wrong, and how I could be

a better person as a result of the experience. It was an interesting and peaceful time. I learned that I could have done some things differently to improve the relationship; that I was selfish at times, not allowing my guy to fully be who he wanted to be for me; and that there were some red flags I had overlooked in order to continue the relationship. It was a wonderful time of growth in my life.

As part of my time of reflection, I decided to plan my first solo vacation. I had plenty of experience with girls' trips, ladies' nights, dating different guys, and being in relationships that focused on being with someone else. This trip was going to be about and for me! Where would I go? I crossed off all international locations because I wasn't comfortable traveling abroad alone. I didn't want to go back to a place I had visited before. It came down to one location that I had always wanted to visit—Boston! I realize Boston may not seem glamorous to everyone, but I have always loved Boston accents, and sometimes it's not about the destination ... it's about the journey.

My Trip to Boston

I booked the flights and hotel and created a loose agenda so I would have plenty of stuff to do, but also have time to let the day get away from me and travel aimlessly. Two short weeks later, I was on a plane to the East Coast.

I must admit that the day before I was scheduled to leave, I was tempted to cancel the trip at the last minute.

Work was very busy, and I'm sure the idea of heading out alone played a part in my thinking about canceling as well. But I knew I would regret it if I didn't get on the plane so I pushed through those insecurities. When I arrived in Boston, I had my route planned to get to the hotel via the subway, and I found my way fairly easily. I love to plan so I had written out detailed instructions for what train to take to what station, and also had a walking map to assist me if I got lost.

The people in Boston were very friendly, so if I had to stop and ask for directions, it wouldn't have been difficult to get someone to help me out. I arrived in my hotel room, unpacked my things, and sat for a few minutes taking everything in. Here I was all by myself in a hotel room in Boston! I didn't have anyone to answer to, I had no responsibility for the next couple of days, and I didn't have to be anywhere by a certain time. I felt a kind of freedom I had never felt before.

Being Alone

Although I had lived alone for more than half of my life, there was something unique about the experience. It felt different being away from my home, where pets, bills, work, phone calls, neighbors, family, and friends could interrupt at any time and potentially require something of me. I was away, and free of almost all responsibility.

It took me a little longer to get settled into the room than I had anticipated. I second-guessed whether I should take a few things off my agenda for the first day, but I decided to head out to see how much I could see. I made it to Harvard University and fell in love with the campus grounds.

My thoughts drifted from college life, to how young and innocent all of the college kids were and how much life they had to live, to the serious professors who briskly walked through Harvard Yard to make it to their class on time, to my ex-fiancé, who had attended Harvard; I could easily see him fitting into this campus setting. I watched the tourists photograph the university campus and famous buildings, and I realized that my thoughts had the freedom to drift in many directions without the distraction of having to engage in conversation with a travel partner.

Traveling alone allows for a long period of self-reflection and provides an opportunity to learn so many new things about yourself. You don't have any distractions, so your mind fills with random, insightful thoughts all focused on wherever your mind decides to take you at a given moment. I grabbed a bite to eat before heading out of the area. My waiter was a six-foot-five African American in his late thirties or early forties, and we mildly flirted back and forth. It didn't lead to anything, but it was nice to be noticed, and I think that being alone makes you more aware of who's around you. I also think guys are more confident about approaching a woman when she's alone.

My next stop was the Museum of Fine Arts and I'm glad I saw it, but it wasn't where I spent the majority of my time. The artistry was amazing, but I learned that I'm not the kind of person who likes to spend hours at a time in a museum. I wasn't as interested in spending time reading about artists and their works as I was in getting to know Boston and the people in it.

Meeting New People

Next stop was Fenway Park. I knew I would be uncomfortable going to a game by myself so I had researched some local bars near Fenway that were supposed to be good hangout spots. Being able to do things alone requires practice. I had gone to a movie alone and had eaten in a restaurant alone, but I hadn't worked my way up to attending a sporting event alone. My first stop was Jerry Remy's, where I met a couple who were just meeting for the first time. They literally had gotten to the bar an hour before I did, and I could tell from their conversation that they didn't know each other well and there was some awkwardness between them.

The woman excused herself to go to the restroom and the guy asked me where I was headed. He said he had noticed my walking map, and he was originally from Boston, so he offered to help direct me to my next location. I told him I was from Chicago and checking out some local hangouts near Fenway. The woman came back, and it was clear she was trying to feel out the situation. I immediately described the conversation to her and we both explained the reason we had started chatting. She was very cool about it.

She offered some advice about places to go and things I should check out. Then the two of them introduced themselves and she said, "We're just meeting for the first time." I told her I thought that was the case and we had a few laughs. It was nice to be able to share conversation with them and be an outsider watching their first date without the pressure of having to be on one myself. I left after sharing a drink with them. I wanted to give them their time to get to know each other.

Exploring

The next day my agenda consisted of the Public Garden, Walk to the Sea, Faneuil Hall Marketplace, the USS *Constitution*, and Bunker Hill. I wasn't sure if I would make it to every place, but it was a comfort to know I had more things to do than time to kill, especially since I was alone.

As I was walking through the Public Garden, I was distracted by so many things going on: vendors selling merchandise and food, performers working for tips, locals catching some rays, and tourists armed with cameras and tour guides. The sounds of lively conversations, birds chirping, engines roaring, and sirens filled my ears. The smells of waffle cones, grilled onions and hot dogs, fresh air, garbage, and exhaust filled my nose. The ambiance reminded me of Chicago, but on a smaller scale.

I hit all my planned destinations that day, had

walked too many miles, and found my way to a restaurant for dinner. After a quick bite, I went two doors
down to a local bar. The vibe was perfect. It had a dive-
bar feel, music was playing on the jukebox, and locals
were hanging out. I met a couple of older guys from
Michigan having beers and New York–style pizza, and
we ended up chatting for a while. It was a great way
to end the trip.

Empowerment

Planning a trip by myself was empowering. It gave
me the luxury to do whatever I decided to do at any
time. I didn't have to take anyone else's opinion into
consideration, I didn't have to worry about checking in
with someone at a given time, and I had the freedom
to explore at my leisure. If I wanted to spend ten hours
of my day at the museum, nobody cared. If I decided
to walk aimlessly through the city all day and let fate
dictate my course, I had the luxury of not having to
plan. I would encourage anyone who hasn't planned
a trip alone to do it. You won't regret it.

My short trip away hadn't filled the void created
by my recently ended relationship, but it instilled
confidence in me. I knew breaking up had been the
right choice and that now the door was open for new
possibilities. I now had a level of self-confidence that I
hadn't had before.

Carrie's Story

Carrie was married to Brad for many years. They had a good marriage, but anyone who has been married for a long time knows that newness and excitement tend to fade in relationships over time. They were committed to each other, loved each other, and had a comfortable life. They were both getting ready for retirement and enjoying their grandchildren. Then one day Brad unexpectedly passed away, and Carrie was put in the position of figuring life out alone. She had her children and grandchildren as a support system, but taking on all of the financial and household responsibilities was a challenge.

Almost ten years after Brad had passed, Carrie was now comfortable in her single life. She was financially stable, working part time, and enjoying time with her grandchildren. Her life was very full and she was content in many ways. She wasn't looking for love, but was open if the opportunity presented itself. She had been on a few dates here and there, but nothing that seemed promising or long term. Then on her way to a meeting she ran into Tom, a classmate from college. They chatted for a while, briefly caught up on old times, and exchanged phone numbers to stay in touch. He and Carrie had been very good friends. They had another mutual close friend and the three of them had spent a lot of time together studying and hanging out. Their personalities clicked, and what Carrie liked most was that they were already friends: she could just be herself and not worry about how she looked, or whether she sounded smart enough or was funny enough.

She found out that Tom had been divorced and was now single. He was living in St. Louis and she was in California so dating wouldn't be easy, but they definitely had more than just a friendship. Carrie enjoyed the idea of exploring the possibility of a new relationship without any pressure. She got butterflies when she heard Tom's ring tone. She felt young again, but more importantly, she felt confidence in herself. They had known each other a long time and even though they hadn't always stayed connected, there was a familiarity that gave her comfort.

Carrie had been through a lot in her life, and she had never really imagined having to date again: the awkwardness, the feel of being interviewed on a first date, checking to see if there is any chemistry, being disappointed, letting the other person down, all of it. It seemed exhausting to her, but this new relationship was different. It was comfortable and felt easy. She wasn't worried about impressing Tom. He already knew her personality, her sense of humor, and the way she looked so she could just move right into enjoying their time together rather than having to filter through all of the normal things she usually would have to do at the beginning of a new relationship.

She and Tom are currently dating long distance, and Carrie is enjoying the freedom of being single and all of the excitement that a new relationship brings.

Joys of Being Single

You shouldn't look to guys to build or boost your self-esteem. You should be grounded in who you are, know what you have to offer, and not let anyone devalue that truth. I've referred to the book *Be Your Own Matchmaker* by Patti Stanger before in this book. I love it because it made me take the time to do a little bit of self-reflection and get to know myself better. Once I gained a clearer perspective of the things I like about me, and the things I didn't like that much, it made it easier to navigate a plan and make some changes. One thing Patti recommends is creating a list of things that make you happy, your top ten. These things or activities can include other people.

For instance, I like playing Texas Hold'em. Obviously, you need a few other players to make a live game interesting, but it's something I really enjoy and I can play online or at the casino alone. I also like traveling for pleasure. This is typically more fun when you are with someone, but as I've pointed out in this chapter, you don't always need a travel partner to make the trip enjoyable.

Assignment

- Make a list of things you like to do. These activities may be things you can do in a relationship, but you don't need to be in a relationship to do them.
- When you have spare time, refer to your list and schedule a few of these activities. You will be amazed at how refreshing life can be when you simply take the time to do things that you really enjoy.
- List the top ten things you like about yourself. Write them down and keep them handy so you can refer to them often.

We live in a superficial world that focuses too much on how much someone weighs or how pretty their face is, so it's sometimes hard to look past the unattainable and realize that we are all awesome in our own individual ways for one reason or another. Being confident in who you are, accepting your attributes and flaws, and loving yourself—that's not wrong or arrogant. It's the way we all should be. We shouldn't allow the voices of anyone in our lives, or in the media, to dictate our value. Take some time to focus on you. As I heard someone say, "You are the best version of you, and nobody else can be you."

What lies behind us and
what lies before us are
tiny matters compared to
what lies within us.
—Ralph Waldo Emerson

12

Embrace Being Single ... and Believe in Life After Love

Do you have any favorite childhood memories? Do you ever reminisce about the good old days? One of my favorite memories from when I was a young girl is of our annual "spring cleaning." Now, let me clarify that cleaning isn't my favorite thing to do, but there is something about having everything in its rightful place, the smell of "clean" in the air, and the idea of a fresh start. Spring cleaning for my family meant the windows in our house were swung wide open, music was blasting from the stereo, and everyone pitched in to ensure that the house was clean and in order.

Part of spring cleaning, as Midwesterners, was the annual clothes exchange: moving the winter wardrobe out of our closets and the summer wardrobe back in.

For me, spring cleaning has always been an upgraded version of regular cleaning because it is a time to put away the feelings of winter, being stuck in the house, and wearing layers and layers of clothing. It is a time of getting ready for the warmth of summer, flowers in bloom, and a new, lighter wardrobe. One of the reasons spring cleaning feels so good is that it usually involves getting rid of a lot of clutter.

Ending relationships can be similar to spring cleaning. During a relationship, we tend to gather a decent amount of clutter through our experiences and emotional connections to that other person. When we end a relationship, we may not realize the amount of unwanted clutter that remains. We may have heavy baggage in our hearts, widespread evidence of bad decisions, signs of a broken heart, and a flood of memories that are hard to clear from our minds.

After my devastating experience in San Diego, I had to be intentional about how I ended that relationship. The hurt was so deep that when I returned to Chicago I made the decision to cut things off completely. The first few weeks back in Chicago were difficult. I knew I had made the right decision, but it wasn't easy. About a year after I moved back, my ex and I tried to reconnect on the phone, but the trust had been completely broken and we realized any type of relationship would be impossible. It can be tempting to go back to an ex because the relationship is familiar, but I'm not sure it ever works out; after all, there was a reason you broke up in the first place.

Part of my de-cluttering after that relationship ended was to work on my ability to trust and love again. I had been so disappointed that it was easier to just assume that people would always hurt me and to keep my guard up—easier than letting it down and risking being hurt again. Disappointment is often part of our lives because not every good thing lasts forever. Being human, people disappoint us. Unfortunately, it's usually the people we let in the closest and love the most who hurt us the worst. They may not even do it intentionally, but we all make mistakes.

To protect against getting hurt, I had built emotional walls so high that they kept me from the freedom to genuinely give love and be loved in return. The process of tearing them down took longer than I expected, and opening myself up to love again required me to step out of my comfort zone. But getting our hopes up, experiencing love, a first kiss, the spark from the touch of a hand, and gazing into each other's eyes can't happen unless we allow the good to come inside. There is a delicate balance between protecting ourselves from being hurt and being open enough to love again.

Although I had dealt with disappointments, broken relationships, and a great deal of hurt in my life, I eventually realized that the wiser choice is to have loved and lost than never to have loved at all. I figured out a way to be content and have a life filled with positive energy and good things. My experience in San Diego taught me a great deal. It's not always easy to let the baggage of the past go and allow yourself to be vulnerable again, but it's the only way you will have the opportunity to find true love. You can't keep walls in place and defense mechanisms fully activated and expect love to overcome them.

Self-Improvement

You may realize that your physical appearance changed during the course of the relationship and your look isn't as fresh as it used to be. Be open to changing up your look a little if that makes you feel good. Sometimes a new haircut or color can do wonders for your self-image. Get back to the gym if you haven't been in a while. Go on a shopping spree and get a new outfit or two. It's important to feel good about the way you look. When you are self-confident, it makes you more attractive and creates positive energy when you interact with others.

One key to ensuring that you successfully move on after a breakup is to remove any and all evidence that reminds you of the relationship. I'm not suggesting you move out of your apartment or to a new city, but you certainly need to return any of your ex's items that are still in your possession. Any gifts that he gave you and photographs that make you think of him should be removed from plain sight. You may want to move everything into the back of your closet or to a friend's house or a storage unit, but it is vital to make sure that anything and everything that reminds you of him ... is gone. The reason this is important is that those items can remind you of all of the good times and you may be tempted to go back to him. Just remember: if he was Mr. Right, you wouldn't have had a reason to break up with him, or he wouldn't have broken up with you. Contentment is being happy and fulfilled with what you have, even if you don't have everything you want.

New Ways to Spend Time Alone

Now that you aren't spending all of your time with your ex, you may find that you have a lot of extra time on your hands. It's essential to have time alone to reflect on your breakup and the things you learned from the relationship, but you have to be careful about how you manage this time. You don't want to spend a lot of time thinking about all of the good aspects of your past relationship and not reflecting on the bad. You also don't want to spend too much time thinking about all of the negative, turning your alone time into an outlet for depression and sadness.

Your alone time may not be sitting in your bedroom in complete silence with a pen and pad of paper in hand, journaling your thoughts. It may be taking a long walk on the beach while listening to your favorite upbeat music. It may be going to the gym for an intense workout that leaves you feeling strong and powerful after those endorphins kick in. It may be sitting in a park watching kids play, dogs run, or a father teaching his son how to play baseball. It doesn't matter what your picture of alone time looks like; it should just be a time when you have the opportunity to fill your soul with the things in life that make you happy. The only requirement is that you aren't using others to fill the void. Instead, you are relying purely on yourself to make you happy.

Girl Code

The fun part of being single again is having the opportunity to reconnect with your girlfriends in a way that wasn't possible when you were in a relationship. It's normal to want to spend all of your time with your new guy at first. It's new, it's exciting, he gives you butterflies, and the potential for love abounds. Dating a new guy can definitely be more stimulating than hanging out with girlfriends, but you want to be careful not to allow a new relationship to make you completely abandon all of your friends.

Most girlfriends understand and will tolerate a friend blowing them off from time to time or not being able to spend as much time with them because they are dating a new guy. But some girlfriends completely neglect their friends and then expect them to be ready, willing, and available to hang out again after a breakup. Be thoughtful about maintaining all of your relationships even when dating someone new so you have girlfriends who are still willing to be there for you when you need them.

It's also important to understand what purpose your girlfriends serve in your life. If you're feeling depressed about your breakup and need someone to listen to how you are feeling, you probably don't want to call your "always ready for a party, drunk and crazy" girlfriend. She may not be the best listener at a time when you are really sensitive and need someone's full attention. However, if you need to have a fun night out and meet new people because you're tired of constantly having the breakup on your mind, she's the perfect girlfriend to call.

It's not selfish of you to rely on your girlfriends during this time. If they are truly friends, they will understand and be there for you. The best girlfriends are the ones who have gone through breakups and not only sympathize with how you are feeling, but can empathize. They will check in on you at different times just to make sure you are doing okay, drag you out of the house when you've been moping around in your PJ's all weekend, plan a girls' night out so you can meet new guys, and maybe even plan a girls' weekend getaway to remove you from your familiar surroundings.

Fun To-Do's

After a breakup is the perfect time to check some things off of your bucket list and cross off some of those goals you have planned for your life. You may have always wanted to go skydiving or bungee jumping. You may have thought about taking a cooking class to improve your skills in the kitchen, considered going back to school to get a degree (or second or third), or volunteering at a local shelter. You may want to get a second job to add a little money to your savings account and have the opportunity to meet new people. There are so many different things you may be interested in — dance classes, sailing lessons, art school, traveling, gardening, pottery classes — so make a list and have it handy for when you need to fill some time slots in your newly open schedule.

When you are single, it's also the perfect time to learn how to be content even if you are alone. If you're someone who doesn't like to do things alone, I challenge you to do just that. Start with something that's not too intimidating for you, like going to the movies alone. This may feel odd at first, but it's the perfect stepping-stone to doing something alone. Once you are in your seat, the lights dim and you have the perfect distraction of watching a movie to forget the fact that you are sitting by yourself.

Intentionally Being Alone

If you master going to the movies alone, step up your game and go to a bar or café alone. This requires some knowledge of your local bars because you want to make sure you aren't the only one sitting at the bar and there is at least one TV in view that can provide a good distraction. Try to make sure you go during a time when you know it will be crowded enough for you to be able to strike up a conversation with someone sitting next to you, but not so crowded that you can't find a seat at the bar. The bartender can be an easy go-to person to start a conversation with and help you feel a little bit more comfortable. Having a drink or two will also help you relax. Guys are much less likely to approach a group of women at a bar, so if you are sitting there alone you are much less intimidating, and it's the perfect opportunity for guys to strike up a conversation with you.

One of the hardest challenges I've had to overcome is eating alone in a restaurant. It makes me feel the most vulnerable because restaurants are usually filled with people who are socializing and enjoying food together; it's not a normal environment for being alone. But there are many people who travel for work and find that it's necessary to eat alone—it may not be their choice, but they do it. Other people choose to eat alone and it's perfectly acceptable. Keep this in mind when you are ready to face the challenge of eating alone in a restaurant. It may not be the norm, but if you can overcome this challenge, you will experience a whole new level of self-confidence.

Some additional tips for eating in a restaurant alone: Like choosing the right bar, you need to be thoughtful about the restaurant and the time you go. I wouldn't recommend going to the most popular restaurant in your area on a Friday night at 7 or 8 p.m. You want to go during a time when other people are there but it's not fully packed while you are the only one sitting alone. Think about going during lunch or early evening. A few other recommendations to make this a challenge you overcome with ease are to ask to sit by a window so you can people-watch, to choose a table for two (sitting at a table for four can make it even more obvious you are eating alone), and to bring some good reading material. You don't want to keep your eyes glued to your phone or be so caught up in reading your book that you miss the experience of dining alone, but you do want a few backup options in place if you start feeling very much out of your comfort zone.

Once you feel comfortable doing some things alone, it will be easier not to hold on to relationships that aren't good for you. You will likely begin to enjoy doing things alone, and may actually choose to even when you have the option of being with friends. It's extremely empowering for women to know they are capable of being alone, and more importantly, being alone and content.

Assignment:

Key things to keep in mind after every breakup:

- Take some time to reflect on what you may have done differently in that relationship, what you wouldn't change at all, and what you learned from the experience.
- If you are having trouble filling your time, make a list of all of the things you've always wanted to do. Make three different lists: 1) things to do alone, 2) things to do with girlfriends, and 3) things to do on a date.
- Reconnect with your girlfriends in a way that wasn't possible when you were in a relationship.
- Check some things off of your bucket list and cross off some of those goals you planned for your life.
- Take the opportunity to learn how to be content even if you are alone.

Doing some emotional spring cleaning after a breakup can be very cleansing. It allows you the opportunity for healthy reflection, honesty, acceptance, and the willingness to change what didn't work in the past. It's a great time to do a refresh, to better understand who you are, and to take some steps to better yourself in an effort to become the best version of you. Be honest with yourself and decide not to allow any of those unwanted behaviors to ruin future relationships.

When you recover or discover
something that nourishes
your soul and brings joy, care
enough about yourself to make
room for it in your life.
—Jean Shinoda Bolen

13

Determine Your Own Fate
... and Plan Your Future

D o you believe in happily ever after? Would you require a prenuptial agreement to get married? Do you have the mind-set that if you aren't happy in marriage it's not a big deal because you can just get a divorce? The divorce rate in America is 40 to 50 percent and the divorce rate for subsequent marriages is even higher. These statistics, and my own parents' divorce, didn't provide me with an optimistic outlook on marriage. I desired to get married, have children, and enjoy a family of my own, but I wasn't assured that my outcome would be marriage until death did us part.

Marsha's Story
Marsha has an amazing relationship with her husband because she can trust him. He's very laid-back, and she

tends to be a bit on the crazy side. She first knew him as a friend, which helped a lot when they started their relationship and she wanted to get to know him at a different level. She really enjoys the way they get along. They are a good team and work well together. They pick up each other's slack when one of them is down. It's significant for Marsha that she can trust her husband. She recognizes the value in being able to have trust in her marriage and she's grateful they have established it. Marsha is confident in her relationship because she feels secure and knows that her husband has her back. She's very comfortable with him and it's because they knew each other for a long time before they started a relationship. They have two kids and he is a very good father, which makes her love him even more.

Her husband is silly and can be goofy. Marsha can be that way as well. Her husband also knows how to deal with the emotional roller coaster she experiences from time to time, and he still thinks it's cute when she cries while watching a movie. Marsha and her husband are still happily married, and she's proud that she took the time to qualify him first, before taking that giant leap of marriage.

Leslie's Story

Leslie is currently single, but during her last relationship, she was a Christian and it lasted about seven months. When she started dating him, they didn't take the time to become friends first or have the chance to see that they weren't compatible. They both put their best foot forward and this made it difficult for them to see that they weren't a good match. Had they spent more time as friends in the beginning, Leslie thinks it would have been much clearer to both of them that they didn't suit one another. Still, one thing she really appreciated about her ex-boyfriend was that he set some very high standards and defined boundaries. He wasn't willing to cross certain lines. In one sense, Leslie felt as if he was too strict and maybe had too high a standard.

Over the course of seven months, he never took the level of their kissing to anything more than a very brief peck on the lips. She respected his boundaries, and it was refreshing to date a Christian for the first time and to experience what those boundaries looked like coming from a guy, but she wouldn't have minded a kiss that was a little bit more intimate. Still, Leslie didn't let this small part of their relationship bother her too much because she enjoyed the feeling of being treated well, respected, and esteemed.

Janet's Story

Janet is happily married. She admits that in her younger years, some qualities and characteristics may not have seemed important to her. But now she knows she wouldn't be able to remain with someone who had a different political view, who didn't share her sense of morality, or who was at odds with her over any other important, fundamental values. She wouldn't be willing to tolerate a racist, sexist, or someone who wasn't open-minded. Her partner would have to be allied with her at a very fundamental level in terms of defining what's good and bad, and would need to possess positive characteristics such as generosity and human decency.

Janet has no plans to get a divorce because her husband has all of the qualities she is looking for, but if she found herself in a position to date again, she would definitely need to assess that potential guy's core values; it is really critical for her. It doesn't mean they have to be a copycat of her, and it's not about hard religious dogma. It's about the human family and whether a guy contributes to it or not.

Fran's Story

Fran is happily married and believed from early on in their relationship that she and her husband were meant to be together. She believes God wanted them to be together; it was more than her wanting to be with this guy. This is the longest relationship she's ever been in. He's fairly conservative, and sometimes Fran tends to be a little on the wild side, wanting to try new ventures in life. Even though he may not always agree with her ideas, he's always been really supportive. About six years ago when Fran wanted to open up a clothing store, he gave her five thousand dollars from his business to get started. He may have thought it might fail, but he was willing to let her give it a shot. As it happened, they did end up closing the store after a couple of years because it was a ton of responsibility and their kids were pretty young and required a lot of their time.

A few years ago, Fran decided she wanted to go back to school to finish her degree. Even though there is a cost associated with that, as well as time away from the family, her husband has been on board with that plan too.

Fran recently had an eye-opening experience: she realized that her husband had been through a lot but had never taken any of it out on her. He has bad headaches almost every day yet he doesn't let it affect the way he treats her. There are certain things he does, like any guy, that can be annoying, but he never tries to take advantage of Fran. He's never gotten physical with her and he's never threatened her. He doesn't try to overpower her and that is very important.

Fran may see a lot of shortfalls in him, but she genuinely appreciates the husband that he is to her. They do fight sometimes and Fran admits that they even dislike each other at times, but they try to work through their issues and problems to make the marriage successful. Fran knows they are both in the marriage; neither of them is leaving so they know where they're both headed. They aren't one of those couples who call each other every day or say, "I love you" all the time, but they work through things well together.

All of these women's stories show that it's possible to be happily married and also possible to be single, happy, and content. It took me a long time to believe that either option could be true for me in my own life, but I feel a new sense of freedom in knowing that either one of them is viable. My faith has been renewed that good relationships do exist and even though they may not be the norm, when you hold out for Mr. Right and sift through all of the wrong guys, you really can enjoy a fairytale happy ending.

The Importance of Financial Stability

A very important aspect of being single and happy is to be financially stable. I've seen so many women who have gone through a divorce and ended up with very little, or who stay with guys they know aren't good for them because they don't have the financial resources to live independent of anyone else. I made the decision early on that I would always be financially independent. I wanted the freedom to be a stay-at-home mom for the first few years, until my kids were old enough to go to school, and I never wanted to feel like I was relying on someone else to meet all of my financial needs.

I started working at the age of thirteen and had a part-time job through my high school years. I didn't go to college immediately after high school, and when I secured a full-time job, I decided to keep a part-time job as well. Having two jobs kept me busy and put more money in my pocket to do the things I wanted to do. I moved out on my own at the age of eighteen, and looking back now, I see that doing that was a big step for someone so young. But it created independence in me that I very much value today.

Moving to San Diego and returning to Chicago created some financial setbacks and at first I was living paycheck to paycheck. But within a few months, I landed a great job and started working on getting my finances back in order. I was also establishing my career and professional life. I took pride in my work, had a solid work ethic, and never let my personal issues get in the way of being professionally successful.

When I broke off my first engagement, I decided to go to college. I was thirty-two years old and was nervous about the experience, but it felt like the perfect distraction and an opportunity to better myself. I had a full-time job that I couldn't leave because I had to pay my bills so I challenged myself to complete one semester attending class full time while working full time. This required working from 8:30 a.m. to 5:30 p.m., Monday through Friday, and then attending class four nights a week from 6:00 to 9:00 p.m.

It was not easy, but I managed to get through the first semester. I kept this pace for the next five years and also figured out a way to complete a required 225-hour internship before graduating. This was a challenging time because my schedule was so hectic, but the learning experience was life changing.

The college I attended regarded social justice highly so most of my classes had a thread of social justice woven through the coursework. In addition to obtaining an education in marketing and communications, I learned so much about equality, human rights, and the people who fought to bring civil rights to our country. Having a degree has given me many new career opportunities, but the valuable information I learned through the coursework opened my mind and heart to a better way of living. I appreciate the wealth of knowledge that I have today from the years I spent in college. It took five years of hard work, discipline, and dedication, and the drive to never give up, but it paid off. I felt proud to walk across the stage and accept my degree. It empowered me in a way that I would not understand until later in my life.

I also obtained a real estate license because I thought it would be the perfect job: I could manage my own hours, and if things ever got too busy, I could always hire an assistant or refer the work to another broker. I've had my license for more than a decade and it's been a huge asset. The additional income has allowed me to pay off almost all my debt and do some traveling.

Another part of my plan to be financially independent was to purchase investment properties. I started off small by purchasing a two-flat home so I could live in the top unit and rent out the first floor. I made upgrades the first few years to increase the value and then eventually decided to add another rental unit in the unfinished basement. Purchasing the property was the best decision I've ever made, and my cost of living is extremely low because most of my mortgage is being paid by the tenants. I plan to continue to purchase investment property in the future to secure income for early retirement and provide assets for my future.

Even though not all of my heart's desires have been fulfilled in the timing I originally expected, I'm optimistic that they will be. My contentment comes from knowing that I'm doing all I can to allow love into my life and be open to finding Mr. Right. Even though my desire to get married and have children didn't pan out the way I expected in my early or late thirties, I didn't put my life on hold waiting. I continued to work toward my goal of being financially independent. I went to college to obtain a higher level of education and expand my horizons. I traveled often to learn about other cultures and see countries I'd always wanted to visit. I've filled my time with hobbies, lessons, classes, and volunteer opportunities to continue to grow as an individual. I've continued to make improvements in my life and to learn from experiences that have made me a better person.

Some days were not easy and there were times when I broke down, asking the same questions every single woman who wants to be married asks when they reach their thirties, forties, or fifties: "Why haven't I found my husband yet?" "What's wrong with me?" "How come all of my friends are married and I'm still single?" But I encourage you to not lose faith, stay hopeful, and trust that it's not you. You are beautiful and deserve to be happily married.

When the time is right, your Mr. Right will sweep you off your feet. The important thing to remember while you are waiting is to focus on you and do everything in your power to create the best version of you so that when your Mr. Right does come along, he has someone whole and content who loves exactly who she is.

Assignment:

To become whole and content on your own, you will need to set goals. Setting goals can be overwhelming, so start with something easy and work your way toward the more difficult items on your list. Take the time to establish a goal or two for the next year. Where do you want to be one year from today? Think about your personal life, your business life, the city you want to live in, what type of property you want to live in, what you want to drive, how you want to dress, or how much money you want to make. Think about things that are important to you that you want to keep in your life or add to your life.

Create an outline or a map of those goals and then write down some ways you can accomplish them. Set a timeline for what goals should be completed by what dates so you can track your progress as the year goes by. If you fall short of one, don't get discouraged. You obviously want to do your best to make the goals you set, but don't let a bump in the road hinder the progress of your year-long journey.

Along the way, as you accomplish some goals, reward yourself—it will help motivate you to continue. Once you have established your first year's goals, it's time to move on to five- and ten-year goals.

Setting five- or ten-year goals is more challenging, but think about what you want out of life. Here is a list of questions you can ask yourself to help generate some ideas:

- What will make your life easier?
- What will make you a happier person?
- Where do you see yourself living?
- How would you like to change or better yourself?
- How would you like to spend your free time in the coming years?
- What can you do in the next five to ten years to ensure financial security?
- What steps can you take to have the career you want?
- What fun things do you hope to accomplish over the next few years?
- Where would you like to travel?

- If you've started a family, what are your goals for your family?
- What can you start doing now to prepare for your future husband or family?

When you create your list you want to be as specific as possible. Your goals should be tangible so you can clearly understand whether or not you have achieved them. Being a better person is a good goal, but it would be hard to determine whether you achieved it if you didn't clearly define what it meant for you to be a better person. Also, identify the most important items and make those your first priority. Selecting a few important goals will help you think specifically about subsidiary goals for each item.

For example, if your goal is to graduate college in five years, your goal over the next few months may be filling out applications to various colleges and getting financial aid in order so you'll be ready to register for classes when the next semester comes along. Make a separate list for each item and plan out a course of action and timeline for each goal so you have a clear picture of what you will need to complete to accomplish that goal.

Translate your long-term goals into a series of short-terms goals that you can accomplish, in order. If you want to travel to ten different countries over the next five years, you may need to do some extensive research to figure out costs, places you want to visit, how much time you are able to get off work, and people you may want to invite to join you (and what their schedules will allow). Use realistic timelines. If you want to run the Boston Marathon, you might give yourself a time frame of a year or two instead of trying to fit that into a short-term goal.

Take time to celebrate each win and realize you are getting that much closer to accomplishing a life goal, so treat yourself to something special. Pay attention to what new objectives arise as you complete each goal; five-year plans can be a moving target. The job market can change drastically and quickly, and the more you move up the job ladder, the more you'll learn what it takes to succeed. A couple of years ago,

it might have seemed straightforward
to get a job as a lawyer in five years, but
once you're deep into law school, you'll
have a better sense of what really needs to
happen.

Periodically amend your list of goals
to take into account these new observa-
tions and goals that come up. Revise your
five-year plan to account for new information. This isn't a failure! It's a sign you're
learning more and getting closer to your
objectives.

FOLLOW *your* DREAMS, THEY KNOW *the way*

14

Realize Your Dreams ... and Appreciate That They Are No Longer Your Nightmares

Do you know anyone who is genuinely happy most of the time—the type of person who has figured out a way to enjoy their journey and live in the present? Such a person isn't focused on what happened in the past, what their future will hold, or how their lives would be better if they were given different circumstances. They have learned to live each moment to its fullest, and they value all of the good in their lives. Whether we are single or in a relationship, learning how to appreciate all that we have is a great way to find happiness.

When we shift our focus away from all the things we don't have and instead focus on what we do, we realize that our cup is half full, not half empty. Even for those of us who may be struggling with great difficulty in life, there is always a positive to hold on to. If you have never done it before, I challenge you to think only about the positives in your life. I guarantee this will create a significant difference in your outlook on life.

Ellie's Story

Ellie was molested as a child by her father and then abused by her first husband, who was an alcoholic. She had a different set of expectations for her second husband. Fortunately for her, she took her time, qualified all potential guys, and ended up marrying the love of her life.

When she met her future husband, she had three daughters from her first marriage. She had a great deal of responsibility and had to work part time to support her family. Working as a waitress, she had to bring her daughters to the restaurant with her because she couldn't afford a babysitter and they were too little to leave home alone.

There was a guy who regularly came into the restaurant for his evening meal. At the time, he was a confirmed bachelor. He noticed Ellie's three little girls sitting in a booth while she was working, and how well behaved they were, and he started to pay attention to her and the kind of person she was.

Given Ellie's history, she wasn't interested in dating and wouldn't give him the time of day, but he was kind to her. She wasn't scared when he was around and her girls noticed the difference in her behavior. After eight months of visiting her in the restaurant, he asked if he could walk Ellie home. She told him he could walk anywhere he wanted—it was a public sidewalk. After a few more months, another waitress at the restaurant invited Ellie and this guy to a wedding and this time Ellie allowed him to walk her home. He saw her to her door and they said goodnight, and he told her he would like to meet her girls. When she said yes, he started taking her girls for ice cream, trying to be their friend first. This allowed the girls to relax and learn to love and trust him. It seemed to Ellie that he wasn't as concerned about impressing her as he was about impressing her girls. Soon they had ice cream together every Sunday, and finally, he won Ellie over.

Ellie agreed to take another walk with him, and as they walked, she was honest with him. She told him that she had never met a man she could trust so she wouldn't be very good for him, and that there was no future for her at all as far as marriage was concerned. He told her he didn't think that it was fair to the girls for her to raise them without a father and not be able to invest the appropriate time she should as a mother.

When Ellie told him she couldn't afford to take her children anywhere, to get them all out of the house, he took the whole family for a ride. He started doing this often to show how much he cared for her girls and to help Ellie get out of her regular routine.

During one of the times they were alone (which

were rare), Ellie told him how she felt about marriage and love. He told Ellie that if she married him and he couldn't show her the difference between love and lust, he would simply take the role of boarder in their house and help her raise the girls that way. He also said he would never ask anything of her until she was ready.

Eventually, she agreed to marry him. And he did teach Ellie the difference between love and lust. He was the first man who made her feel like a woman. He knew about her background and understood how much healing she needed before she could respond to him.

He was a great father and a good provider, and the kids loved him. He was understanding, but also firm. He didn't give in to the kids to make them like him. He was caring and let them know he loved them. Even though they weren't his, he raised them as his own. He wasn't just a "father" to her girls. He was closer than that, a "daddy," and Daddy is what they always called him.

Ellie and her husband were married for thirty-four years before he passed. She thanks God for him every day, and is happy knowing that what he saw in her life led him to know God too.

Jessica's Story

Jessica is happily married now, but not all of her past relationships were good. She'd had abusive relationships and through those experiences decided she was going to let God choose the next man for her. She knew that God knew what she needed and desired and He ultimately provided the best relationship and marriage she's ever had. Her husband is not perfect, but he's the closest to perfection of any of her relationships.

First and foremost, he loves God more than he loves Jessica and that is extremely important. In her opinion, how he relates to God is an indication of how he will relate to her. He's kind, trustworthy, faithful, and extremely honest. She feels safe with him. In her opinion, he's always "easy on the eye," and she's told him he always reminds her of Clarke Gable. He replies that she's got rose-colored glasses on, but Jessica really loves the way he looks: his height, the massiveness of his hands, his eyes, and his boyish, impish smile. She likes that he can be very serious but can do "high-school like" things too. He likes to tease her and it keeps things young in their relationship.

Another thing Jessica loves about him is that he can fix almost anything. He's a "handyman special" and this is especially important to her because they own investment property. He's very clean too—at home and when he's fixing their investment properties. He's a man of integrity, and he respects Jessica. He lets her know he loves her in his own way. He doesn't always say, "I love you," and he's not always mushy, but when he says it she knows it comes from his heart. Every now and then he'll say, "You know, I love you" or "You're a good wife," and it really touches Jessica's heart because she knows he means it.

He's not a romantic kind of guy with spoken words

so he goes out of his way to find greeting cards that say what's in his heart. He chooses beautiful ones, and they always tell Jessica how much she means to him. He's an excellent lover, and a part of her knows the reason they are so compatible physically is that they waited until they were married to have sex and God honors that. It seemed odd to some that they had both been married previously and yet still decided to wait until they were married to consummate their marriage, but Jessica shared it was worth it!

If he is jealous, she's only seen it once in all the years they've been married and it surprised her. He seems secure in himself and he doesn't appear to have any insecurities related to her. If he has them, he doesn't show it or let her know.

Another really important thing is that Jessica knows he would never abuse her—verbally, emotionally, or physically. He'd walk away before he would say or do something hurtful—literally walk away from the situation and cool down. He was the first man who helped her look at a relationship beyond the physical, helping her realize that a serious relationship is so much more than that.

This was a different dating experience for Jessica; he was the first guy she dated as a Christian. She had to make some adjustments in herself and view the relationship differently. It was a challenge for both of them at times, but they both agreed that there wouldn't be any intimate physical relations until they were married.

Jessica thinks women who have good father figures and can ask for their honest opinions have a much better chance of understanding the proper way for men to treat women, and can better recognize abusive behavior when it happens. The woman may not want to hear what her father has to say, or she may be embarrassed to share her personal life, but he might give her the good, sound advice she really needs. Men know men and how they think. Jessica believes that a woman who has the opportunity should at least ask her father relationship questions because dads love their daughters and most would be willing to share how they feel about a situation and offer advice.

A woman can ask God to let her know if a potential guy is right for her. During the time Jessica was single, God placed four men in her life. They were all put there to help her experience being with a man without the physical overtones of being in an intimate relationship. They became friends and they just hung out together. The guys shared male things with her, something she had never had before. Looking back, she realizes that God knew it was important for her to see men not as potential partners but as regular people, the same way she saw her girlfriends. She needed to understand and appreciate this perspective before getting into a serious relationship again. It was an eye-opening experience for her.

Jessica thinks women tend to settle when they are waiting for the right guy. They get anxious and end up going for the wrong guy instead of taking time to find the right one. She wants all single women to trust her from her experience: the right guy is well worth the wait.

Sharon's Story

When Sharon was younger, she didn't care so much about the quality of the guys she dated, but when she was looking to get married she knew she had to qualify any potential guys to ensure she would have a happy and successful marriage. She felt it was important to make sure they were stable and wanted to have kids. It was also important that they got along with her family since that would be a big part of their lives in the future.

Something else that was important to her was that the guy wanted to buy a home one day and not always be happy living in an apartment. This wasn't necessarily about the cost of the house or the guy having a lot of money, but that he wanted to settle down and build a foundation. It was important to Sharon to find someone with similar goals in life and to agree on how they would spend their money. Sharon tends to be cheap when it comes to spending, and she's diligent about saving money, so she wanted any guy who could possibly become her husband to value spending their money wisely as well. She looked at his work ethic to see if he was disciplined and worked hard.

Sharon took the time to qualify all potential guys and now has a husband who is very reliable and responsible. He has his priorities straight and he's mature enough (they are both mature enough) to make the marriage last. They both know that they need their individual space as much as their time together, and Sharon thinks it's good that they each have their own space. They both have their own friends, but they still take the time to date and spend time together as a couple.

When you are smart enough and strong enough to lose the wrong guy, you put yourself in a position to be happy and focus on fulfilling your dreams. The stress, drama, and day-to-day struggle of dealing with the wrong guys are gone. Your time is freed up to dream, hope, and have faith in what your life can be today.

Hope

Hope is a powerful feeling that can drive people to do amazing things. It has the capacity to heal and it can motivate people to do the extraordinary. Hope can make the impossible ... possible.

Amelia Earhart had a desire to fly, and through the power of hope, her fiery personality, and dogged determination, she became one of the first female pioneers in the aviation industry. In her mid-thirties, she married George Putnam, who was helping her prepare for her solo flight across the Atlantic. She was adamant about retaining her independence and referred to their marriage as a "partnership" with "dual control."

In 1932 she made her first attempt to fly across the Atlantic, and although weather conditions caused her to land prematurely, she managed to fly 1,750 miles (just 750 miles short of her goal). Shortly after her success, President Herbert Hoover presented Earhart with a gold medal from the National Geographic Society. Her continued hope inspired her to try to be the first woman to fly around the world. When she was thirty-nine years old, Earhart and her navigator departed from Miami and began the 29,000-mile journey. By June 29, when they landed in Lae, New Guinea, all but 7,000 miles had been completed. On July 2, 1937, they took off for their next hop to Howland Island. Their communication was interrupted by static, and weather conditions were inclement. Earhart's last communication was heard at 8:45 a.m. on July 2, 1937.

Earhart's bravery and hope pushed her to make the impossible ... possible. She received many awards during her lifetime and Amelia Earhart awards and scholarships are given out every year to honor her memory and unwillingness to give up. In a letter to her husband written in case a dangerous flight proved to be her last, her brave spirit was clear. "Please know I am quite aware of the hazards," she said. "I want to do it because I want to do it. Women must try to do things as men have tried. When they fail, their failure must be but a challenge to others."

Amelia Earhart was an inspiring female entrepreneur who allowed love into her life but didn't let it limit the way she lived. She knew that her hopes and desires were just as important as her husband's and they made an amazing team working together to make both of their dreams come true.

I hope this story inspires you and makes you dream for the impossible. Whether in your life or your relationships, keep hope and faith alive, and never give up on your dreams.

Contentment and Faith

Faith is another very powerful force and, like hope, can make the impossible... possible. It is something I've learned to develop through the years, based on my trust that God has a better plan for me and that His ways are higher than mine. I may not understand the circumstances I face or the reasons some of my desires are not fulfilled in the time frame I anticipate, but my faith has kept me content each and every day. It is what has motivated me to continue to improve who I am and the quality of my life. My story may seem insignificant compared to Earhart's, but when we have the power to influence our own lives, and the lives of those around us, in a positive way, that is a huge testament to who we are and the choices we have made for our lives.

I've gained a life filled with contentment and fulfillment because of the decisions I have made. I have an amazing family, I have some of the best friends anyone could ask for, I have a great job, I'm financially secure, and I'm in the perfect place to find Mr. Right.

The nightmares of my past no longer haunt me. The drama I once had in my life is no longer present and I will never allow it back in. I'm smart enough now to recognize the wrong guy and am capable of keeping him out of my life. I'm proud to have arrived.

If you take the appropriate steps, you will find you can be content with what you have and love who you are. These things are not out of reach—they are possible for you! My hope for you is that you realize your dreams, experience the fairytale, and never let the wrong guy back into your life. May you have faith and trust that even though you may not see him today, Mr. Right is searching for you and will find you at just the right time.

You must do the things you
think you cannot do.
—Eleanor Roosevelt

Notes

Chapter 3
Pp. 40–41: "... to become that person." Scott H. Young, *Decide Who You Want to Be*, May 2006. Accessed 11/8/17.

P. 43: "... respond to it that matters." Epictetus (55–135 C.E.), *Internet Encyclopedia of Philosophy*. Accessed 11/8/17.

Chapter 4
P. 61: "... in no longer trying." Elbert Hubbard, Goodreads. Accessed 11/8/17.

Chapter 5
Pp. 63–64: "... had over their own bodies." *The Evolution of Dating and 'Pick-Up' Guides*, Shaping the Unconventional Path, 11/16/14. Accessed 11/8/17.

P. 64: "... legalized abortion nationwide." *Roe v. Wade*, Findlaw. Accessed 11/8/17.

Pp. 63–65: "...high school sweethearts." *History of Dating*, SexInfo. Online. Accessed 11/8/17.

P. 65: "... reached their mid-twenties." Yvette Caster, *15 ways dating was different in the 90s*, Metro News, 3/18/15. Accessed 11/8/17.

P. 65: "... seemingly endless options." Victor Verdugo, *The Main Differences Between Dating Now vs in the 2000s,* Popsugar, 4/26/16. Accessed 11/8/17.

P. 74: "... before becoming intimate." Steve Harvey, *Act Like a Lady, Think Like a Man* (New York: HarperCollins Publishers, 2009, 2014).

Pp. 73–76: "... make the first move." *50 Dating Dos and DON'Ts,* Glamour. Accessed 11/8/17.

P. 77: "... like the chase." Patti Stanger, *Become Your Own Matchmaker* (New York: Simon and Schuster, 2009).

P. 81: "... achieving our mark." Michelangelo, Goodreads. Accessed 11/8/17.

Chapter 6
P. 97: "... to do what is right." Rev. Dr. Martin Luther King, Jr., Assembly Speaker at Oberlin College, October 26, 1964.

Chapter 7
P. 100: "... remove the blame of." Dictionary.com. Accessed 11/8/17

Pp. 111–12: "... he checks out." Kim Quindlen, 25 Easy-To-Miss Signs That You're With The Wrong Person, Thought Catalog. March 4, 2015.

P. 113: "... other life but this." Thoreau, *Walden.* Favorite Thoreau Quotes, Thoreau-Harding Project. Accessed 11/8/17.

Chapter 9
P. 147: "... valley of change." Shannon Adler, Goodreads. Accessed 11/8/17

Chapter 10
P. 163: "... try, try again." William Edward Hickson, BrainyQuote.com. Accessed 11/8/17.

Chapter 11
P. 177: "… what lies within us." Ralph Waldo Emerson, Goodreads. Accessed 11/8/17.

Chapter 12
P. 191: "… for it in your life." Dr. Jean Shinoda Bolen, Goodreads. Accessed 11/8/17.

Chapter 13
P. 193: "… marriages is even higher." *Marriage and Divorce,* American Psychological Association. Accessed 11/8/17.

Pp. 203–7: "… closer to your objectives." *How to Write a Five Year Plan,* Wikihow. Accessed 11/8/17.

Chapter 14
Pp. 217–19: "… challenge to others." Biography, Amelia Earhart.com. Accessed 11/8/17.

P. 221: "…think you cannot do." Eleanor Roosevelt, BrainyQuote.com. Accessed 11/8/17.

Illustration Credits

About the Author

Renee Medema, a Chicago native who studied integrated marketing communications at Roosevelt University, is a marketing manager for a law firm and a real estate broker in the city. This year Renee has had the opportunity to serve as a mentor in the Year Up program, sharing career and life advice and learning from her mentee. For the past ten years, Renee has also partnered with Breakthrough Urban Ministries in East Garfield Park, assisting with their efforts to build community and help those in need achieve dignity and opportunity.

In her free time, Renee enjoys traveling, dining out at new restaurants, investing in real estate, riding her Can-Am motorcycle, and spending time with family and friends.

This is Renee's first book, and she would love to hear directly from her readers. You may contact her at renee@howtolosethewrongguy.com.

CPSIA information can be obtained
at www.ICGtesting.com
Printed in the USA
FSOW02n1854070218
44307FS

9 780999 522318